HOW TO
PASS
EXAMS

HAMLYN HELP YOURSELF GUIDE

HOW TO PASS EXAMS

C.M. HILLS

HAMLYN

Acknowledgements

The publishers wish to thank Macmillan Publishers Ltd.
and G.B. Buckwell for kind permission to use the extract from
Mathematics CGSE — Cruise Through Exams

First published in 1989 by
The Hamlyn Publishing Group Limited,
a division of the Octopus Publishing Group,
Michelin House, 81 Fulham Road,
London SW3 6RB

Printed and bound by The Guernsey Press

Contents

Introduction

Everyone has to take exams at some point in their lives. And nowadays they have to take more of them. As competition becomes stiffer for jobs, school leavers and graduates have to get more and better exam results. Often extra vocational training is demanded, with additional exams to be taken. Exams don't even necessarily end when you leave school or college – many jobs involve exams that must be passed along the way to gain promotion.

Yet it is a truth universally acknowledged, that most people dread exams. It's not only first-time GCSE takers who get worried – mature students who have had jobs, produced families and run companies can turn to jelly when faced with an exam paper and a three-hour deadline. Nor is it only people who don't know their stuff that are affected like this. Students who have conscientiously completed all the work and are very well prepared can panic even more than those who haven't and aren't – because there is more at stake.

But panic is the worst enemy you can have when it comes to taking an exam. It prevents you from preparing and ties your brain in knots when you are trying to write the exam. Douglas Adams's *Hitchhiker's Guide to the Galaxy* had on its cover, in large friendly letters, the words 'DON'T PANIC'. That is also the message of this book. And remember, if you are only taking an exam, you have far less to worry about than Adams's unfortunate hitchhikers. After all, the world isn't about to end and you are not threatened with extinction by green Vogons!

But it's easy to say 'DON'T PANIC' if you haven't got an exam coming up. You may be thinking, 'How on earth can I stop myself panicking?' This book aims to drive out fear with knowledge. It's not knowledge of the subject you need at first, though this will be essential later on – it's knowledge of the exam that you are taking, knowledge about yourself and knowledge about how to combine the two to the best effect. In other words, STRATEGY.

☐ *You can be as clever as you like and still fail if you don't know what will be expected of you.*

The most important element of working for exams is your frame of mind. Keep confident – you *can* do it. You wouldn't be on your course if somebody didn't think you could do it. Feeling that you can't do it immediately makes you unable to do anything. Your brain feels paralysed and you can't think straight. If you tell yourself that you can do it, you can then start thinking about the easiest and most successful ways to get it done. This book will show you how to discover these ways – but it can't do much for you unless you really believe in yourself. Think positive and you will get positive results.

Perhaps one of the most positive ways of approaching an exam is to see it not just as a dreaded hurdle, but as relevant in a number of ways to ordinary everyday life. Among other things, an exam tests a number of skills: your ability to sum up a situation, to express yourself clearly, to come to the point, get the facts right and state them concisely and efficiently. So learning how to tackle an exam successfully can also come in useful in all sorts of situations outside the exam room, wherever skills like these are required. And although very few people can truly say they *enjoy* exams, there is certainly considerable satisfaction and a sense of achievement to be gained from knowing that you have done your very best. That is what this book will help you to do.

The first half of this book should be seen as a survival kit. It will teach you:

- How to find out about the exam you are taking – the questions you need to ask and where to find the answers.
- How to take your own character into account when you are working.
- How to plan a revision campaign.
- How to put it into practice.
- How to cope in the exam room.

Everyone should read this half of the book. If you've only got a short time left before your exam, that's probably all you will be able to read. But if you do have more time, the second half, entitled

'Some Further Tactics', looks at more specialized sorts of exam and gives hints on how to answer different sorts of question. There is also a chapter on coursework and one on how to make sure you are looking after yourself properly. Flick through this half and then read those sections which apply to you.

Everyone is different, and this book aims to help anyone taking exams – school and college exams, external exams such as GCSEs and A-levels, diplomas, professional exams, university finals or whatever. So I have included information on different sorts of question and different sorts of student. But the central point of this book is that passing exams is to do with strategy – and although your strategies may vary, the way you decide on them won't.

The language in this book is simple. The last thing you need at this stage is another long complicated textbook to read. I will call the people teaching you 'teachers' throughout – although your college may call them tutors or whatever – and will call you 'students'. Don't feel patronized by this at all – it's just to make things easier. And don't be put off if your situation is different – if you are teaching yourself, for instance. You will be able to see as you go along what will apply to you.

Use this book. As you read through, fill in the answers, try the examples, join the dots. Make it fit your situation by writing in the details of *your* exams. It's you it's meant to be helping. As you revise, use all the information you have written in. Then when you have finished your exams, you can chuck it onto the bonfire if you like!

One final point. Despite the best campaigns and strategies, exams, like wars, still call for some luck. And that's what this book wishes you.

Good luck!

Part One
A Survival Kit

1

Knowing the Exam

Before you even start to revise, you need to know quite a lot about the exam that you are revising *for*. This is because:

- If you don't know what it covers, you can't choose the right subjects to revise.
- If you aren't aware of a continuous assessment element, you may pass the exam papers but fail on your coursework.
- If you don't know what *sorts* of question you will be expected to answer, you can't practise doing them.
- If you don't know how many questions you have to answer, or from which section, you will waste valuable time in the exam room working it out.
- If you don't know how the exam paper is structured, you may waste time on unimportant questions when you should be doing others which carry more marks.

If you are to be tested, you need above all to know exactly *what* your examiner will be testing you on. An exam doesn't just test whether you are clever. How could it? Intelligence takes so many different forms that one exam could never test it. Rather, your examiner will be trying to see whether or not you have a certain set of skills. Can you jump through the right hoops? The first step on the way through those hoops is to know what they are. This may sound rather cynical, and certainly there is room in exams for originality. But before you can get through your hoops with flair and daring, you must know in what direction you have to leap.

> □ *An examination is a test of your skills. It's not intended to label people as clever or stupid.*

How much do you know about your exams? Here is a quiz to help you find out. Be honest with yourself. If you don't know the answers, don't panic. You will find advice on where to find them at the end of the quiz. Remember, this quiz may well be the most important exam you ever take!

Quiz

All questions are compulsory. You have as long as it takes to answer them in full.

1. Do you know whether your course assessment is based entirely on your exams? .... Yes/No

If other work apart from exams is assessed on your course, answer Part A:

PART A

2. Do you know what percentage of the total mark this work carries? .... Yes/No

3. Do you know how many assignments you have to complete? ...
Yes/No

4. Do you know if there is a choice of assignments? .... Yes/No

5. Do you know if you can choose how many you submit? Yes/No

6. Do you know when each has to be completed by? .... Yes/No

7. Do you know what happens if you do not complete an assignment by the deadline? .... Yes/No

8. Do you know if you can discuss an assignment with the teacher and revise your original draft before the final mark is awarded? ...
Yes/No

If you have to take written exams, answer Part B. Remember that you need to know these things about *all* your exams.

PART B

9. Do you know how many papers you have to take for each subject? .... Yes/No

10. Do you know which topics each of your exam papers will cover?
Yes/No

11. Do you know if there is a choice of papers you can take? Yes/No

12. Do you know which papers you are taking? .... Yes/No

13. Do you know if you can choose which questions to answer? ...
Yes/No

14. Do you know how many questions you will have to answer on each paper? .... Yes/No

15. Do you know if any of the questions are compulsory? . . Yes/No

16. Do you know if any of the questions are divided up into parts?
Yes/No

17. Do you know if you have any of the following types of exam?
Yes/No

   a) A multiple choice exam
   b) A 24-hour paper
   c) An oral exam
   d) An aural exam
   e) A practical exam

18. Do you know how much time you have to answer each question? .... Yes/No

19. Do you know if some questions carry more marks than others?
Yes/No

20. Do you know if you are expected to write in full sentences or in note form? .... Yes/No

21. Do you know roughly how much you are expected to write altogether? .... Yes/No

22. Do you know how long the exam lasts? .... Yes/No

23. Do you know if you are allowed to take books, your notes, scientific tables or calculators into the exam? .... Yes/No

How did you do?

This is one exam you can mark yourself – plenty of people will be busy marking you in the near future! How did you do?
Score one mark for each question that you knew the answer to.
Write your score here. . .(Part A). . . . .(Part B). . . . . . .

What was your result?

Less than 5 in Part A or Part B

However much you may know about your subjects, you need to learn more about the ways you will be examined in them. It's just a waste of all your hard-earned knowledge if you don't know how you are going to be asked to apply it. You are risking losing a lot of marks needlessly – if you don't know what the paper will look like, you may be taken off your guard, get in a panic and answer the wrong number of questions or something equally silly. Get in the know quickly – the next section of this chapter will help you to do this.

A few questions you couldn't answer in Part A or Part B
You are reasonably well-prepared to start your revision campaign. But before you do, find out the answers to any questions you couldn't answer. You need all the information you can get *before* you start if you are to revise sensibly and save time.

Full marks
Congratulations, superstudent! Now you know all about the exam, it's time to find out some things about yourself. Turn to the next chapter.

If you scored a low mark you may be feeling that you can't possibly do all this research about the exam and revise for it! Don't despair – if you didn't already know the answers to these questions, it is usually quite easy and quick to find them out. And this is work that will eventually cut down your job and make life easier and more relaxed for you.

Remember also that this book is written for people doing all sorts of exams. You need to see where it applies to you and steer your course by that.

Ways to find out about the exam

1. The easiest way is to ask your teacher
He or she is probably the one guiding you through the whole business. It is your teacher's job to know what you have to do. Teachers will be very familiar with the whole process of exams, and have access to examiner's reports which give extra guidance on those places where students tend to slip up.

Make sure that your exams are not too far ahead when you tackle your teacher. If it is very early on in your course, your teacher may feel that you are worrying too much, and advise you just to stick to what you are learning in class. To look at a whole syllabus when you are just beginning a course can be alarming, when in fact you would feel quite happy about it two years later when you have had time to get to grips with it. And at this early stage it is often better to cover the topics in the wide-ranging way that is possible in class, rather than just trying to answer specific exam questions, designed to be tackled in a very short period of time.

But sometimes teachers can leave talking about the exam until far too late. If you feel that you do need to know more about what is expected, or you are learning outside the classroom, there are other ways of finding out.

2. *Looking at old exam papers*

This is perhaps the best way of finding out what yours will look like. You should obtain past papers for at least the last three years. First make sure that you know the right exam board, the exact name of the subject and which syllabus you are taking – there may well be more than one. Then contact the board to find out where to go to buy past papers. You will find a list of exam boards and their addresses at the end of this book – ask your teacher if you can't find yours there.

When you look at a past paper, don't worry if you find you don't know the answers to all the questions straightaway. It may be that they are on topics you haven't covered yet, or topics that you have, but heavily disguised. Anyway, you are highly unlikely to *need* to answer all the questions in any case, as it is rare for papers not to give you a choice.

If you are taking GCSE exams, you are slightly at a disadvantage here in that there are fewer papers available, as the exam was only introduced recently. But don't despair. Use all the old papers that you can get hold of, and then ask your teacher to make up some similar types of question for you, especially on areas you are less good at.

If you can get past papers from several years back for your course – and these can usually be obtained very cheaply in booklet form – check whether each paper has the same format. If you are basing revision on old papers, you want to be very sure that they are the same as yours will be, or at least that you know what will be different.

3. Find the syllabus

Syllabuses are available from the board which sets your exam, but they can be so filled with either/or clauses and technical jargon that they are sometimes difficult to understand. However, if you feel that your teacher has abandoned you, you may want to obtain the syllabus, if only to get him or her back on track. If you are worried that you aren't covering the course properly in class, get together in a group and ask your teacher about what you will be expected to do. He or she should give you a list of the topics that are to be covered, especially if it's fairly near the exam.

4. Ask people who took the exam last year

They can be a great help, perhaps sometimes being a bit more on your wavelength than your teachers. Ask if anything was different from what they'd expected, and what they found difficult. Elder brothers and sisters can be helpful here. But beware of people trying to scare you with horror stories – or the opposite, those who have just forgotten that it was difficult at all!

Now use these methods to answer any of the quiz questions you couldn't do originally. Use the quiz as a checklist.

You are now ready to go on to the next section of this book which will ask you some questions about yourself. Now that you know what the exam is like, you need to know what *you* are like.

2

Knowing Yourself

You shouldn't just plunge into a revision campaign without thinking a bit about yourself first. For instance, if you know you tend to be lazy, it's not good strategy to plan to work eighteen hours a day. You won't be able to do it. Remember that everyone is different – you need to find out what *you* are like and plan accordingly.

This section will ask you to take a look at your strengths and weaknesses. Be honest – it is more useful to you in the long run. But don't get depressed – remember your strengths as well!

Your weaknesses

Here are some work problems that you might be prone to, and that most of us are at some time. Don't worry too much about them – just tick them if you recognize something that you tend to do. Then read the hints that follow on how to combat them.

Do you procrastinate?
A long word for putting off getting started. Everyone tries to put off starting work, because work means thinking and concentrating, which is hard. The ways people find to put things off vary, but perhaps the most common is a ploy known as 'whitening your tennis shoes'. The phrase comes from a character in Lynne Reid Banks's novel, *The L-shaped Room*:

> *Have you ever tried to write? It's the most bloody business. Any excuse is good enough to get away from the typewriter . . . Did you ever hear the story about the man who was commissioned to do a piece for the Saturday Evening Post? . . . Well, he needed the money, he wanted to do the piece; he had a deadline to meet, but he kept putting it off. Any excuse not to get started. He missed two deadlines and the third and last was set*

for 1 January. On the last night of December the Editor rang him up and said was it ready? No, not quite, said this character, he was just going to start it but first he had to clean his tennis shoes.

It's all too easy to find yourself whitening your tennis shoes in this way before a revision session. Do you use any of the following activities regularly to put off work?

- Domestic activities: cooking meals for the next week in advance, hoovering the carpet, going to the launderette, or doing all the washing up before you can start.
- Getting ready for revision: sharpening ten pencils, going to a stationers and buying more notebooks, lots of different coloured pens and other items or rearranging your bedroom before you can start.
- Over-organizing your notes: setting up a card index system or computerizing the lot before you can start.
- Extracurricular activities such as sport, or music or drama: pretending that they must be done before you start.
- Talking to friends: 'I must just have a chat with John about the essay before I start'.
- Reading too many books on how to pass exams . . .
- (You probably have a delaying tactic of your own. Be honest – write something down)

Whitening your tennis shoes isn't the only way to put off work. Here are some others:

The 'plenty of time yet' trick
Saying that there is plenty of time left, you needn't start now. This one can go on indefinitely.

The clock trick
Saying that you will start work at 10 o'clock, or if you are still drinking your coffee when it comes to 10, at half past. Round numbers seem to have a magic attraction when it comes to delaying tactics.

The 'I work best under pressure' trick
A subtle one this – it involves trying to convince yourself that you will be able to do things more quickly and efficiently if you are under pressure.

The 'just another ten minutes snooze' trick
It's especially easy to procrastinate when starting work also involves waking up. I have dreamed that I have written whole essays – and then woken up.

The 'I need to do more reading before I can start the essay' trick
This one is closely bound up with perfectionism. Sometimes you can find yourself putting off doing the real work by doing other unnecessary work.

How not to procrastinate
It is very hard to stop putting things off, especially if you have that sort of character. But it can be done! Here is a three-point plan for getting down to things:

1. Recognize that you are putting things off
You may think that this sounds silly, but many people get so good at procrastination that they don't even realize when they are doing it. Think carefully about all the tricks which are listed above. Do you use any of them, or any very similar ones? The deadly thing about some of these delaying tactics is that any one of them *might* be a thoroughly genuine reason to delay starting – you might really need to do some more reading before you start, for example. You need to recognize when you are putting something off for a really valid reason, and when you are just being lazy and you can't bear the thought of starting.

2. Recognize the disadvantages of putting things off
The longer you put something off, the more unpleasant the thought of actually doing it becomes. And you don't enjoy the time you are not working because you are worrying about what you are going to have to do. When you finally get round to it, you will probably be too near the deadline to do it as well as you know you could have done it or to get any satisfaction from it.

3. Get started!
Everything seems easier once you have made a start. At worst, you may find that you have problems – but at least you will be starting to solve them. At best, you may well find that the task wasn't as difficult as you feared.

Do you get distracted?

Have you had the experience where you start full of good intentions to revise, and then you find that you want a cup of coffee and go and make that and then the kitchen is full of your friends and you start talking and then you go back but you find you haven't got the right file and have to get that and then you need an extra jumper and then the phone rings . . .

Try to avoid basic human needs cropping up when you start a revision session. Make sure that the room is warm enough, that you are not hungry (exam time is no time to start a diet), that you have water and/or coffee and tea to hand and that you have been to the lavatory. Make sure that you have all the textbooks, paper, pens and notes that you will need *before* you start. Keep your mind off sex and anything else that's irrelevant! Try to have a parent, or friend or answerphone on hand to field your telephone calls – you can ring people back *after* you have finished the session. The best way to avoid distraction is to be organized.

Do you watch too much TV?

Do you spend all your time in front of the box and none at your desk? Perhaps without enjoying much of what you watch? Don't allow yourself to watch TV indiscriminately. Restrict yourself to particular programmes – never turn on the set unless you know what you want to watch. Never watch TV before your revision session, always leave it for a treat afterwards.

Are you taking too much on?

Are other duties pressing in on you, such as school duties, sport, music or other outside interests? Or are you studying part-time and have domestic responsibilities or a demanding full-time job to cope with? Do you find that you are under constant pressure to get everything done?

Work out how important the other responsibilities are to you, and how you could get rid of them if they are less important than your exams. Remember that you can always start them up again afterwards – there is life after exams! It is important to see the exam period as temporary. But don't leave yourself with nothing but exam work – you will need breaks for different activities. Try to strike a happy medium. Just make sure that you don't join three football teams or arrange to take a holiday immediately before your exams. If you are studying part-time, try to get domestic help if possible, from friends or relatives or family. Explain to your family that your exams are important. They don't want you to fail and have to go through the whole performance again next year.

Do you daydream?

Once you have started revision, does your mind wander off and start thinking about what you are going to do that evening and then you wake with a start and find it's fifteen minutes later and you've read the same page eight times?

It's very hard to stop daydreaming completely. The chief thing is to notice when you are doing it. Then you can try to pull your attention back to the matter in hand. Activities like taking notes, making lists, asking yourself questions or automatically trying to recall what you have taken in at the end of each paragraph will help you to avoid daydreaming. Give your mind plenty to do, then it cannot escape. Try to minimize outside worries when you are taking exams – do not move house, end a relationship, fall out with your best friend or fall in love. Otherwise you may find it hard to get your brain off these worries and on to your work. You have plenty to worry about already!

Does panic stop you from working?

Do you find that you are reluctant to get started because of the extent of your work? Or do you stop working, paralysed with fear, in the middle of a session because you realize how much more you have to do?

The best way of avoiding fear is to start well in advance and to have a well-planned revision timetable. You will learn how to make this in the next chapter. Then you will be able to tell yourself that everything is covered and that there is no real need to feel afraid. If you have divided up your work, you should be constantly achieving small goals, which is another good way to become more confident.

If despite all these efforts you still find yourself gripped by fear in the middle of a session, force yourself to keep going, at least for the amount of time you promised yourself previously. Make yourself achieve something, however small. Once you have finished the session, talk to teachers, friends or parents who might be able to reassure you. If it gets too bad and you find you are too scared and depressed to work at all, see your college counsellor or your doctor.

Are you too much of a perfectionist?

Do you often feel that you can't finish something because it isn't as good as you'd wanted it to be? Try to set yourself realistic goals for what you can achieve: split tasks up into smaller ones if necessary. If you are stuck, try to analyse what the problem is, and then find a way of solving it. If you are really paralysed, force yourself to write anything, and then see how it can be best organized. If you frequently find yourself unable to complete work because you feel it isn't good enough, have a chat with your teacher to discuss the sort of standard you should be aiming at.

Do you react badly to criticism?

Are you edgy about accepting criticism? Do you get annoyed when your teacher makes comments about your essay? Most people find it hard to accept other people's opinions about their work, especially if these opinions are very negative. If you are feeling unsure about what you are doing anyway, it is very hard to listen when someone else tears it to pieces. And if your critic is someone you don't respect much anyway it is even more difficult.

One good way of dealing with criticism is to put the piece of work aside for a couple of days. Then come back to it and read it as if *you* were the teacher. You may well find yourself seeing some sense in some of the criticisms – it's often hard to see flaws in something you have only just completed. If you still don't agree with what someone says, at least work out why you don't. Your teachers are not just trying to get at you. They are anxious to see you improve and do well and their advice can be very useful. Get a second opinion if necessary, perhaps from another teacher more sympathetic to your work.

Do you ignore subjects you can't stand?

Most of us at some point have to take exams in subjects we don't like. But the less you like a subject, the less likely you are to pass your exam. The temptation is always to leave revising that subject until last. Work out how important it is to you to pass. If it is important, try to find ways of making yourself like the subject more. Think about why you dislike it so much. Is it because you never understand? Take a relatively easy topic and see if you can't master it. Make every effort with this one topic – use your textbook or your teacher, or try to find an easier book on the subject. If you can master some element of the subject, you may find yourself enjoying it a lot more.

Are you badly behind with the coursework? Try to catch up if at all possible. It is almost impossible to enjoy doing a piece of work if you are already very behind with it. If you find just one element of the subject to interest you, you are far more likely to pass.

Are you terrible at getting up in the mornings?

Are you a lark or an owl? Larks are people who do their best work in the morning, but are hopeless later on in the day. Owls will stay up very late to write an essay, but they can't get up in the mornings. Most students are owls, but you may find that you are a lark! Plan your revision timetable accordingly – make sure that you are working at the times that suit you best. When you cannot plan your own timetable and have to attend college classes and lectures, you may need to cultivate more larkish tendencies. You will regret it later on if you sleep through vital classes – and even more if you sleep through your actual exam.

Turning over a new leaf

You should have learned something about yourself by reading and answering these questions. Use this knowledge to improve your study techniques. You can't expect a conversion overnight – there will still be times when you put off work, or daydream or whatever – but you should now be able to cut down on these times. The first step in kicking a bad habit is knowing that you've got it.

□ *Knowledge is power.*

Now you know about your exam and yourself, you are ready to use this information to plan your campaign.

3

Planning the Campaign

Generals fight battles by adopting overall strategies first and attending to the details later. This is the way you should plan your campaign. Computer scientists call it the 'top-down' approach because you start at the top, at a very general level, and then work down to the details.

Here is an example of the the top-down approach in general life. You are planning a busy morning's shopping. First you plan which shops you have to visit and in which order you want to visit them. Then you write down a list of what you want to buy at each shop.

The opposite approach is called 'bottom-up'. Here you would write a long list of things you want and set off shopping. For each item on the list you visit a shop which sells it. In the end you will get all the things you want, but it is likely that shopping this way will take much longer than with a top-down approach – you will probably find yourself visiting the same shops several times.

The top-down approach to your exams
Starting right at the top, the first thing to do is to choose which subjects to take. (If you've already made that decision, ignore this part.) Be careful about how many exams you take in the one year. Your teachers will advise you on this, but most employers or colleges will be more impressed with good results in a few subjects than with a string of low grades. Nobody needs fourteen GCSEs.

Which subjects should you take? Certain subjects, like English, Maths, and sometimes a foreign language or a science, are much in demand both with employers and further education. So check what you will need for your planned next move, and concentrate on doing well in those subjects. If you are thinking of doing a college course, consider the subject you will eventually be learning. Are there subjects that will be useful for it? A lot of science courses will require you to have Maths A-level. Teacher training at present asks for a Maths qualification, whatever subject you want to end up teaching. If you are going to study English Literature, then you might find that French, Latin or History comes in handy.

Think also about the *kind* of subjects you are doing – do they all require you to write long essays and learn files full of facts? Or could you combine them with more practical subjects to get variety? Consult your careers adviser.

Dividing your time

The next thing to do is write down the number of weeks before your exam starts. Make a list of the days between now and the start of your exams and divide each into morning, afternoon and evening. Your table might look something like this for each week:

		Morning	Afternoon	Evening
Mon.	15			
Tues.	16			
Wed.	17			
Thurs.	18			
Fri.	19			
Sat.	20			
Sun.	21			

Divide each morning, afternoon or evening into two sessions. Go through the list and mark all the parts that are already taken up with some engagement. How many free sessions do you have?

You can't work all the time, so you will need to leave some sessions free for having a break and doing something completely different. Someone may invite you to a party you can't possibly miss – always leave some room (but not too much) for temptation. How many sessions you leave free depends on what sort of worker you are, but about three sessions on to one off is a sensible number to aim for.

How many sessions do you now have left for revision? Divide this by the number of subjects in a rough order of priority: at the top put the ones that you know will need the most attention and at the bottom put the ones you feel most confident about. You should adjust the number of sessions per subject and give a few more to the subjects at the top than to those at the bottom. Don't be too mean to the subjects you are good at; after all, you want to do particularly well in these.

At this stage you may have to face up to the fact that you don't have enough sessions per subject. It is hard to decide what is enough, but if you end up with one session per subject, for instance, you will know that you have problems. Here is some advice: see if there are any classes you feel you are getting very little out of attending. Then give up going to them. Use the time more profitably for your own revision. This is tough advice to follow because if you give up going to classes and also fail to revise on your own, you are in big trouble. You shouldn't just cut classes for the sake of it; and don't do it earlier than about three weeks before your exam. But if you do have sufficient self-discipline to succeed in revising in this extra time, and do it well, you will get far more out of it than you would by attending classes. The trouble with going to classes at this last-minute stage is that they use up valuable time without forcing you to do the thinking. It may be very soothing to see that your teacher has the whole subject under control, but this can con you into thinking that you have it under control as well. Now is the time for *you* to act, to think and to work out for yourself why one statement follows from another. Your teacher won't be there in the exam room.

When are your exams? If they are very close, you will need to think about the dates when you make your revision timetable. Remember that oral tests often come much earlier than the main exams, so you will want to start revising for these first. Are there great gaps between exams during which you will be able to revise? Or are they all frighteningly close? Don't fall into the trap of putting all your energy and time into the papers that come first and leaving none for the ones that follow. Remember that you will need more time than usual during the exam period to relax, so don't con yourself that you will be able to do much work in between exams. It is extremely hard to sit an exam in the morning and then sit down to some serious revision in the afternoon – exams are exhausting! And if you haven't done too well in the morning, it is easy to get dispirited by the thought of all the work you still have to do. Use the time between exams usefully if you can, especially if you have gaps of more than three days or so, but never pin your hopes on it. Make sure that you have revised thoroughly beforehand.

Making a revision timetable

You need to take account of what sort of worker you are when making your timetable. Do you study best in the evenings or during the day? Do you hate working at the weekends? Are you a lark or an owl? Bear your own personal preferences in mind when you plan the timetable. You are the one who will have to see it through. A revision plan is as much a psychological tool as an academic one: if you feel that you are constantly slipping behind your schedule, you won't gain any sense of achievement for what you have done, and panic may stop you doing any more.

Take each subject you want to revise and divide it up into topics for revision. There is no hard-and-fast rule for what makes a 'topic', but one guide is that a question on an exam paper is likely to test a single topic and this topic is unlikely to come up again on the same paper. For example, an important topic in Mathematics is how to draw graphs and use them to solve problems. It is likely that any question on graphs will be devoted solely to graphs and unlikely that graphs will come up in any other questions on the same paper.

Check that your list of topics is complete by using chapter headings in your textbook or study guide, or by looking through past papers. Study guides can be particularly useful for this. You should expect to divide each subject into between ten and twenty topics. Most exams divide up into two parts. The first section will test your basic knowledge of all these topics. It will probably consist of simple short questions. The second part will ask for a more detailed knowledge of some specific topics. The questions will be longer and expect you to go into more depth in your answer. Look at your past papers – what sort of questions are they asking?

In an ideal world you would learn every topic in enough detail to be able to answer a longer question on it. But this is not an ideal world and very few students find themselves in the happy position of having enough time to do this. You will need to be selective. As long as you know enough about the whole syllabus to answer short questions (if your exam includes these), you can afford to pick and choose which topics you prepare for your more detailed answers. Remember that it is better to have a few topics you can write about confidently than a lot you are sketchy on. You should try to leave yourself at least one 'spare topic', however – extra ammunition up your sleeve in case your strategy falls flat and one of your topics fails to come up or does so in a form you cannot answer.

A Revision Timetable

	Monday	Tuesday	Wednesday	Thursday	Friday	Saturday	Sunday
Early morning session 9–10.30am	Lessons	Lessons	History Revision	Lessons	Lessons	Maths Revision	Free
Late morning session 11–12.30am	Lessons	Maths Revision	Lessons	Business Studies Revision	Lessons	Science Revision	Business Studies Revision
Early afternoon session 2–3.30pm	Maths Revision	Lessons	Lessons	Games	Maths Revision	French Revision	Science Revision
Late afternoon session 4–5.30pm	Geography Revision	English Revision	French Revision	Games	Geography Revision	Business Studies Revision	History Revision
Early evening session 7–8.30pm	History Revision	Geography Revision	Music Lesson	Free	Science Revision	Free	Free
Late evening session 9–10.30pm	Free	Free	English Revision	French Revision	Free	Free	Free

Now select the topics you want to concentrate on in your revision. If you find this difficult, try the following approach. First chuck out all the topics you have absolutely no hope of passing on. Put them in one pile: these are dead topics. Then take the ones you are good at – healthy topics – and put them in another pile. Do you have enough healthy topics to answer on? If you don't, you need to find some topics in between your dead pile and your healthy pile which you could nurse back to life in the time given, and give more time in your revision plan to these.

If you are very short of time you may want to do some question spotting. This is a dangerous practice – you can never rely on any topic coming up – but you may be forced into it. Look at past papers for the last three years or so, making sure that the syllabus hasn't changed radically since then. Look at all the questions in front of you and decide which topic each is testing. Does one topic come up every year? If so – especially if it is one that your teacher has laid great stress on – you have a fair chance of its coming up this year. Not a 100 per cent chance, however, because examiners know about question spotting. You can also look out for topics that seem to come up fairly constantly – perhaps every other paper. Trying to spot actual patterns, such as the French Revolution coming up every three papers, is foolhardy; exam papers are set by human beings and do not follow mathematical progressions. The last sort of question to look out for is the one that isn't there – the important topic that hasn't come up for ages.

☐ Making a choice of which topics to concentrate on is the most important part of revision. Don't make the mistake of trying to revise everything – you may end up revising nothing through panic.

You have now made your list of topics and can divide the number of sessions allocated to each subject by the number of topics to see how many sessions you can give to each topic. To make a timetable you will have to go back to your list of days and sessions and spread the topics around the sessions. A sample revision timetable is shown on page 28. In the example, the student has allowed more sessions for Maths (his weak subject) and correspondingly fewer for English which he is good at. Before you make your list, however, read to the end of this chapter for some advice on how to do this spreading.

If a topic seems to need several sessions, split it. The more you split up a topic the more manageable it will seem. But keep the parts in order of priority – important things first – just in case you don't get round to doing everything.

Keep revision sessions short – most people find it difficult to concentrate after about two hours. On the other hand, you won't get much done in less than half an hour, unless you have set yourself a short task such as learning vocabulary. An hour with a break of fifteen minutes and then another three-quarters of an hour works well as a revision session, but set your own pattern. Remember to keep your breaks short but frequent so that your brain stays as fresh as possible. Sometimes things that seemed completely impossible before a break will be easy after one. When all else fails, give your subconscious a chance – sometimes your brain can go on working away at a problem even when you aren't consciously thinking about it, and come up with the right answer next morning! Recognize that there will be times when you won't do any work whatever the time of day – because you are tired, or lazy, or depressed, or something else crops up – so build some leeway into your timetable to cope with these occasions.

Try to vary the subjects you are revising. It is much easier to make yourself work for longer if you can split the session up mentally by saying 'That's the maths finished, now I'll do the chemistry.' But make sure that when you have interlinked topics, you revise them fairly close together, as this will help your memory. Vary topics you like with those you don't. Don't be tempted to put the subjects you hate at the end of your timetable. The more you put off something, the more unpleasant it will seem, and it is harder to revise something you find difficult if you are feeling nervous near an exam.

Know which subjects must be tackled early on. Any subject which calls for a progressive understanding – you can't understand the new bit if you don't yet understand the old one – should not be left to the last minute. Maths and languages are good examples of this sort of subject.

Talk to your teacher about what is happening at school. Then you can plan your timetable to fit in with any revision being done in class.

Leave some time at the end to go over everything for the last time.

Now go and make your timetable.

A daily hit list, with items in order of importance

Task	*Estimated time*
1. Finish History essay	1 hour
2. Revise graphs for Maths and do sample questions	½ hour
3. Revise *Othello* notes and try thinking about essay outlines	¾ hour

Remember to cross things off once they have been done!

4

How to Revise

Revision involves practising skills and learning facts. It does not involve going completely through the whole course again and mastering every single bit you couldn't do first time round, however poor a job you may have made of it then. While revising, you do pick up new skills and learn new facts, but only as a consequence of seeing that you need them. As you try to master topics, and attempt new questions, you will see what the gaps are. It is then up to you to fill these – as far as possible in the time you have left. In fact, revision is itself very like a very long exam with no rules. This time, however, *you* are the one who has to ask the questions, not the examiner.

Skills need constant testing as you go along. The only way to do this is to try them out, but start with easy ones! Skills are like muscles – if you try to lift a heavy weight without practising on light ones first, you are likely to end up on the floor. Go back to books and notes you used at the start of your course and use these as a source of practice problems. Don't be too proud to use books which are written at a more elementary level than the ones you have been using. These can be very useful to get you started. Even Ladybird books can be helpful! Study guides are handy too, but make sure they have lots of small questions which test basic skills. Don't go straight to old exam questions, because you are likely to find these too difficult at the start of your revision. Make sure you are fairly confident about what you are doing first – *then* try the exam question.

Learning facts is much easier if you understand them in the first place. Yes, you can get some subjects off parrot-fashion, but it will take longer and be useless to you if an unusual question comes up. You need to see that you have all the relevant facts, that they are well organized and that you understand them *before* you start to commit them to memory. Once an argument or an explanation fits together in your mind, half the job of remembering it is done.

Making a start

Now is the time to marshal your resources. You will already have divided up your time and your topics and matched the two (see Chapter 3). Now you need to see what you have got already in the way of notes and information, and where the gaps are. This is much easier to do now your subjects are divided up into individual topics – you can see what needs special attention. In most exams, having topics you know nothing about doesn't matter too much; there's usually another question you can do. But having gaps within the topics you have decided to revise is much more serious, because there may well be only one question on that topic, and if you can't do that you will be stuck. So don't spread yourself too thinly. It is better to have fewer topics well revised than a host of things you know a little about.

Go through your notes on the topic you have chosen to revise and highlight what seem to be the most important parts – this is where highlighter pens really come into their own. If there are gaps caused by classes you missed or bits you failed to understand, make a note of them. A quick skim through past papers can be useful in suggesting topics you should know about but don't seem to have any notes on. Make a list of all the gaps and highlight the important ones.

Filling the gaps

Your textbook comes into its own at this time, but don't start doing other reading now. It is a bit late to start looking through unfamiliar books, although it might be worth reading a chapter on your topic, for instance, or an article. If you do, use chapter headings and the index to avoid wasting time reading irrelevant bits. Go straight to the section you need – don't get distracted or panicky reading other material. Pass-notes and study guides which break subjects down into essential points can come in very handy at this stage. Time is of the essence, so you will only want to read what is important – get advice from your teacher or better-prepared friends, but don't let them rattle you.

When reading either your familiar textbook or new material,

Which set of notes would you prefer to come back to? This scrawled page, or a neat organised piece of work?

Economics defined by Alfred Marshall - Victorian econ. as "study of mankind in the everyday business of life" drawing attention to the uniq. features of human sc. unlike other animals man provides complex path of production, distribution + exchange. Everyday bus. of providing means of livlihood called by term economics - ~~soc~~ Scarcity study of econ. such as in Europe US. Advanced econs. interest us most. How do we dist. products among groups in sc.? What instit. developed to promote economic activity + how does each instit. play its part in the relationship of everyday life)

<u>Economics</u>   3 November 1988

Mr. Smith

What is economics?

'The study of mankind in the everyday
business of life'. (Alfred Marshall -
Victorian economist.)

Unique feature of human society -
complex pattern of production, distribution and exchange.

Advanced economies (eg. W. Europe
& USA) are the most interesting.

1. How do we produce everything we need?
2. How are products distributed among
groups in society?
3. What institutions have developed to
promote economic activity?
4. How does each institution play
its part in everyday life?

read through the section quite quickly, making a note of the main points. Only include what seems important. Leave out examples. (If they are good ones you will probably remember them anyway.) Remember that you can always put extra material in later – but you don't want to frighten yourself with too much at this stage. Try to keep your notes concise and clear – you will probably want to return to them. Make sure that you understand everything you have made notes about. It is very hard to remember information you don't understand.

If you are really desperate, and have missed a lot of classes, you may have to borrow notes from your friends. Choose the friends who make good notes – they should be easy to read, clearly set out under headings and make logical sense. Borrow from someone who understands the subjects, not just someone who writes down every word they hear. You may find that such notes are rather in demand at the moment. Stress that you only want to borrow them for half an hour, and then photocopy them – money well spent. Teacher hand-outs are also very useful to revise from, especially if they are typed and well set out. It's well worth nagging teachers for hand-outs as exam time comes up.

Now you can arrange old and new notes together, in a sensible order, keeping information on the same topics together.

Have you got too much information?
Are you one of those wonderful people who keep files and files of notes, then wonder how they are going to learn them all? If you are, your problems are a bit different. Careful treatment with a high-lighter pen is what is required. Be honest and sort out what is important. If you try to learn all your notes you will end up knowing nothing, and the sheer bulk of it all will put you into a panic. Make sure you cut down your notes into essential facts. Don't try to learn masses of examples and quotations – stick to a few especially relevant ones.

Once you have a well-organized, clear set of notes it is time to set about learning them. But before you plunge in, here are a few hints to remember about revision in general.

Get organized before you start each revision session
Before starting, make sure that you have all the equipment you need to hand – pens and pencils, rulers and rubbers, coloured pens

and highlighters to make your notes clearer, a ring-binder so you can rearrange notes if necessary and a plentiful supply of file paper to go in it. Don't forget to get any textbooks you will need, and a calculator for scientific subjects. The point is not to be distracted in the middle of a session.

Before you start, map out what you hope to cover in the session. You may or may not achieve this, but try at least to have a rough plan of what you will be able to do in the time. If you divide up your own work into units which are easily achievable, you will feel more satisfied at the end of the session. It is psychologically very important to feel that you have got something done. When you have finished, tick off what you have achieved on your list and reward yourself suitably.

Have a routine for working

Doing anything by routine is much less painful, as you don't think so much about it and it becomes automatic. If you always sit down at your desk at 7 p.m. you won't find it so hard to do so tonight. Do you have strange rituals which make it easier for you to work? These are completely personal, but you may find it easier to work if, for example, you always chant a spell to yourself before you start – or always wear the same jumper for revision.

Choose a good place to revise

You need somewhere warm and quiet to study. This can be at home, or at school or in a library – wherever you feel happiest. Some people like to establish a routine of working always in the same place. This gives them a feeling of security, and the right associations: if you always work at your desk, when you sit down at it you will feel in the mood for work, with any luck! Trying a new place can help if you are turning over a new leaf. 'Now I have discovered this new library,' you can say to yourself, 'I will do lots of work.' But beware of trekking from library to library in search of the ideal workplace. You may find the problem is more to do with yourself.

The advantages of working at home are that you can have everything you need to hand – and if you do forget something, it isn't so hard to get it. You may find that you are distracted by the presence of other people, and like to be on your own. (But remember that you will be surrounded by others in the exam room so know at least that you *can* work with people in the room. Beware of trying to revise at the kitchen table at home – you are bound to be distracted. Try to find somewhere where you can be quiet, and where the surroundings are reasonably tidy which is always a boost to orderly thinking. A chaotic, cluttered room is not usually conducive to the best work.

Libraries and other places of study can have pleasant worklike atmospheres, and you may find that having people studying around you helps you to concentrate. If you want to consult another book, that will be handy too. Working in places far away from home can be useful to avoid distractions and it is sometimes a good idea to make getting home to the TV or friends a bit more difficult. Beware of planning to work too far from home, though – you may never leave your house in the first place. Be careful about how much you take with you to a library – you don't want to lose your whole set of notes. Photocopying essential notes and keeping them separately in a safe place may help to set your mind at rest.

Now you are seated at your desk, with a pile of well-organized notes in front of you, it is time to start learning facts and practising skills.

Ways of learning notes

1. Rereading them. This is a handy way of learning, but make sure you are not day-dreaming and missing the point. Take yourself by surprise occasionally by putting your notes to one side and trying to express out loud the content of the last few paragraphs.

2. Underlining the key points as you read through the notes. Or get that highlighter busy again!

3. Reading the notes out loud to yourself. This is very useful if you have that sort of memory. If you are the sort of person who finds learning poetry easy, this method will probably appeal to you. Make facts into little rhymes if you like – anything that makes them easier to learn.

4. Writing the notes out again. Often a very effective method, but they shouldn't be too long or you will despair. Don't copy out every detail, just stick to key points. This is also helpful if you are trying to sort out a ragbag of notes.

An essential part of memorizing something is testing to see whether you have succeeded. Try to write out the main facts again without looking at the originals. When learning vocabulary, cover up the words in the foreign language and write down the words in English. Do it the other way round too, and don't forget the gender. Get other people to test you on your recall, or have group learning sessions. If you get a few of your friends together and go round the room asking questions, learning can seem a lot less painful. Just make sure you keep to revising and don't start chatting!

Practising on past papers

Get an array of papers in front of you. Papers from the last three years should be enough. First check that you know what is covered in the exam and the structure of the paper. Go back to the quiz on p.12 and use it as a checklist. Make sure that the syllabus hasn't changed and that your paper will look like the ones in front of you. You need to become very familiar with this structure, so you are not thrown by it when you are faced with your own exam paper.

If there is no choice of questions, you should practise doing all the questions on the past papers.

If there is a choice – and most exam papers will allow you this – you need to pick out the topics you have decided to revise and practise the questions on them. Some exams make this very easy and you will be able to turn to 'your' question in the secure knowledge that it will be there, but in others topics may be in disguise or even not there at all. Know which sort of exam paper *you* are taking! Watch out for:

(a) Exams which say you must make a choice of questions from each section. You need to check that you have enough prepared topics to cope with this.

(b) Compulsory questions: e.g. Answer question 1 and three others. If a question is compulsory, revise the topic very carefully: it is obviously important. It is unusual for an exam to set a compulsory question on a completely unspecified subject within the syllabus, so you will normally have some indication of what ground it will cover, or the skill which it will test. The disadvantages of a compulsory question are obvious – if you can't do it at all you will lose marks – but remember the advantages as well. You don't have to use up precious moments deciding which question to answer and can get straight into the work without wasting time.

(c) Questions in parts. If you can't answer the second part of the question, it isn't that much good to you. If your past papers seem to specialize in setting rather unrelated topics within the same question, you will have to prepare more topics.

(d) Questions that seem more easy or difficult than they really are. Questions that appear too easy may contain pitfalls (look carefully – can you really answer all the parts?) or may expect a much more detailed treatment than a harder-looking question. Harder questions may be easier than they look. Think about why you can't do them – is it because you don't have the information (in which case you must decide whether you should try to learn the topic at this stage) or because you just don't really understand what information is wanted? If you don't understand at all what the question wants, do ask a teacher – you can only answer a question if you know what it wants you to say. You will find more about answering questions in Chapter 7.

(e) Questions that carry a lot of marks. You will want to spend more time revising these subject areas.

Now take the topic you are revising and look at the questions that are set on it. Are you in a position to answer them all, including the ones where you think it is your topic that is wanted, but it seems to be in disguise? (Remember that topics won't always appear in exactly the form you expect.) Have a go at some of the questions. If they are short or multiple-choice, try to do them in full. If they are longer essay questions, do outlines and make general notes on the approach you would take, the information you would use and how you would structure your answer if you were doing the question in full.

Doing questions from past papers helps you to see where you need more information, and to revise more thoroughly. Don't worry if there are just a few things you can't do – noone can do everything – but try and fill the major gaps.

Testing yourself and mock exams

It is very important to keep testing yourself on what you know. The more often you can drag a piece of information out of your mind, the more likely it is to spring to the surface when you need it in the exam room. After you study each topic, try to write down or say out loud the key facts about it, from memory. Get your friends to ask you questions. Or set yourself little tests. Go over things a few days later as well if possible, just to check that they are still there.

The next stage is to practise doing questions to a time limit. Writing exam answers is a very unnatural activity, so you will need plenty of practice in doing them. Having a good plan – brief notes of all the important points and how you are going to fit them together – is essential for a good answer, so make sure you practise making a plan for each question. Start with single questions and then work up to a whole practice exam or 'mock', completing a past paper you have not seen before in the allotted time. Keep a paper specially for this purpose. You should try to reproduce exam conditions as exactly as possible. So if you are not allowed, say, a calculator in the exam, check that you can do exam questions without one in the given time. Make sure that you have learnt any formulae or quotations that you would usually look up, if you are not allowed to do this in your exam. And remember that even if you are allowed a book in the exam, it may take too long to look up the relevant table or quotation, so make sure that you are familiar with the layout of the book, and how to find your way around it for what you need. Be strong when you take your mock – don't find an easier exam paper if you are having trouble with the one in front of you.

When you have finished, take a long break. You deserve one. Then come back to your answers. Where did you have problems? Could you answer enough questions? Did you run out of time? You may want to show what you have done to your teacher, who will be helpful in suggesting what you need to work at.

Mock exams at college

Many courses will include this sort of test-run themselves at some stage. Mocks at college can be very useful as they are more like a real exam than anything you can fake yourself, and because you are guaranteed some teacher feedback on what you have done. Look at your results carefully; they will teach you a lot about the realities of taking the exam. Did you panic? Don't worry too much if you do badly in mocks, as your performance will improve with time. Remember that the aim is to find out what you need to improve, not to do well for its own sake.

Some warnings about mock exams
Don't take them too early on. If you don't yet have the information to answer the questions they will be of very little use to you and may be off-putting.

Don't take too many of them. Many schools seem to put their pupils through so many mocks that when the real exam comes round, they can't find the necessary adrenalin to do well – it just seems like another mock.

Don't take mocks too seriously – for good or bad. Don't assume that because you did very well in the mock you will do well in the exam. The real thing may include half as much coursework again – you must be prepared to cover what was taught after the mock. Likewise, don't despair if you did badly: if you use the mock to see where you need to do more work, and where you need to improve your exam technique, you will probably do much better in the real thing.

How to keep yourself revising
Most of us find it fairly easy to plan a revision campaign and to get started. Everyone likes making lists – it is sticking to them which is difficult. If you are finding it very hard to keep your revision schedule, consider the following points:

- Are you setting yourself too much to do? Remember that you can't revise everything. Go back to your original schedule and see if there are things that can be left out without disastrous consequences.
- Are you dividing up your tasks so that you get a sense of achievement for each one completed?
- Are you panicking rather than working? Try to keep going – remind yourself that you don't have to learn everything to pass.

If you feel that it is laziness that is preventing you from working, you need to force yourself to keep going by using incentives – sticks or carrots. If you were a donkey, would you go better if someone dangled a carrot in front of you, or threatened you with a stick from behind? Most students find that carrots work better than sticks, but you may need to try a mixture of both.

Carrots can be straightforward treats, such as the promise of sweets, or a chat with friends, or a night at the disco *after* you have finished a work session. Or they can take a more subtle psychological form such as a free evening without guilt, if you finish the essay by 6 o'clock, or allowing yourself to think of the benefits of exam success – the admiration and envy of all who know you, that coveted college place, the wonderful job, the money, the fame, the power. This is a dangerous one – it's all too easy to start day-dreaming of success in the middle of a revision session. This is called the 'It'll be lovely when it's finished' fallacy and is well known to those starting any sort of large project, particularly home decorating.

Sticks are altogether harsher, but you may need to threaten yourself if you are really being lazy. Tell yourself that you can't go out if you don't finish the revision session satisfactorily. Think of the guilt that will follow if you don't do the work you have set yourself and just think what will happen if you don't pass this exam. Sticks can be dangerously negative – you may get depressed and that will stop you from working too. It depends on your persona-lity. If you know you are likely to worry too much, stay with carrots. But if you are really procrastinating, a stick may be what you need.

Stay cheerful

Your state of mind is the most important thing to consider when taking exams. Be positive! By this stage in the book, you should have worked out your strengths and weaknesses, what you need to improve and what will stand you in good stead. Divide things up; don't say to yourself; 'I hardly know anything about this play', instead tell yourself that you have read Act One, and only have Acts Two and Three to go. Once you have made your master plan, live from day to day. At the end of a revision session, concentrate on what you have done, rather than on what you have to do tomorrow. Reward yourself for small achievements. If you think about the exam, concentrate on strategies and policies – don't just panic vaguely.

Avoid talking too much to friends in the same boat, they will worry you even more. Watch out for those operating the 'I've done no work' strategy. It probably isn't true, and it will certainly distract you from your revision. Also avoid those who claim to have mastered the whole course – this is equally unlikely to be true. Above all, keep cheerful. It may seem like the end of the world and revision is hell, but there is life after exams!

5

In the Exam Room

So imagine that all your well-organized revision is over and it's exam time. What should you do now?

Don't panic

Do try your utmost not to panic. Remember that it's counter-productive – you won't be in the right frame of mind to do your best if fear prevents you from concentrating. If you find yourself panicking before the exam, do something physical: jump up and down or run round the block. Try to avoid those last-minute gaggles of people working themselves up into great states of fear. They're not doing themselves any good and they're no fun to be with, especially if you are really worried.

Just before the exam . . .

Be nice to yourself

Try to give yourself at least a day off before the exam in your revision timetable. Do something completely different to take your mind off it. Sport is often good – go for a walk or a swim, or play tennis. Try to get yourself physically tired so that you sleep well the night before. Don't just go over and over your notes – you probably won't learn any more anyway. And *certainly* don't try to learn anything new – your brain won't have time to slot it into perspective! People vary on how close to the exam they feel they can profitably work, but do give yourself some rest time. Look over your notes beforehand if you must, but do not exhaust yourself. Remember that you have three very hard hours' work ahead and save yourself for that.

Make sure you have registered properly

Check that you have filled out any necessary forms that have to be completed beforehand, and find any required numbers or ID that you will need. Some exams may even call for a passport or special papers – make sure that you have everything necessary.

Get a good night's sleep

If you can. Try anything that works for you; hot drinks (but not coffee or tea or anything containing caffeine) and magazines can work wonders. Sleeping pills should be avoided at all costs: they can make you feel dopey and lethargic next day, just when you need to feel most alert. If you can't sleep too well, don't worry. It won't stop you from working well in the exam as the extra adrenalin will keep you awake. It is amazing how well your body can cope under stress for short periods and you will probably find that you don't notice at all that you need sleep. But do try to get some if you can, if only to prevent yourself from lying there worrying.

Know where you have to be

Make sure you know where the exam is to be held and when, and allow yourself plenty of time to get there and to go through any necessary check-in procedures. You will need to balance this between not leaving yourself enough time – and worrying about being late and leaving yourself far too much and having to spend ages hanging about working yourself up into a panic. Strike a happy medium!

Have the right exam gear

Wear loose comfortable clothes if possible; in bright colours if they cheer you up! Be prepared for the exam room to be either very hot or very cold – take lots of layers.

Get all your equipment ready

Make sure you have everything you will need for the exam ready the night before. Do you have your pencil case (if you are allowed one) with pencils, rubbers, sharpeners, pens, cartridges and all the rest? Take two of everything you could possibly need, in case one breaks. (It won't, but this will make you feel happier.) Take your calculator if allowed, and check beforehand that it conforms to the regulations (calculators are usually required to be silent, cordless and nonprogrammable, but check the regulations your exam). Make sure you have a spare battery. Get ready any books or notes that you are allowed to take into the exam – check whether it is the sort of open-book exam which provides the texts. If so, be familiar with the edition that will be used, or you could waste a lot of valuable time.

Take something to chew on

Sweets or chewing gum (if allowed) can be handy – some people tend to chew the inside of their mouths when under pressure, and you may have other nervous tics, so something to chew can be relaxing. If you feel you need extra energy, glucose tablets can help too, if only psychologically. Make sure you haven't brought anything too crunchy, though – the smallest noise can be infuriating to other candidates and you might get lynched after the exam is over.

Remember your watch

Bring a watch that you can rely on, or a small clock that can go on your desk. Again, two are better than one. Make sure that they are set to the invigilator's time – synchronize them at the start. Steer clear of watches with in-built alarms, you don't want them to bleep at hourly intervals during the exam!

A small request for personal hygiene

Yes, you may have been working so flat out that you haven't had time to wash, but spare a thought for the other candidates. A bath can be very relaxing before an exam.

Go to the lavatory before you go into the exam room

Fear will probably make you want to anyway, but you don't want to be distracted once you are in the exam room.

Once inside the exam room . . .

Choose a good place to sit

If you are allowed choose to where to sit, use this advantage. Make sure if possible that you are far from your friends and people you know well – it is too distracting wondering how they are doing. For similar reasons, it is wise not to be too near the window, especially if there is anything interesting or noisy going on outside.

If your desk wobbles, get it fixed before you start the exam: change your desk or wedge something underneath it. Otherwise half your mind will be obsessed with an irrelevant problem for three hours.

Don't cheat

However foolproof your method seems to be, there is always the possibility that you will be caught. However, the preparation for cheating can be as effective as the cheating itself – all that writing out information on small bits of paper to be hidden in your socks, or inscribing useful facts on unnoticeable bits of flesh can really make the facts stick in your mind. So the moral seems to be: prepare to cheat and then firmly put all the stuff away or wash it off before you get anywhere near the exam. Invigilators are up to all the good dodges. Don't risk it. Remember that doing badly in an exam will damage your career far less than being caught cheating in one. It just isn't worth it.

Obey the exam room rules

Once the invigilator calls for silence, shut up. This may be from the moment you enter the exam room, so be careful. And don't turn over the paper until you are allowed to do so.

Ignore any unavoidable distractions

If there is noise from outside, or a loudly ticking wall clock in the exam room, try not to get upset about it. Once you start doing the questions, you should be so deep into the exam that you will forget about it. I knew one girl who spent almost an hour of an exam asking for a clock to be moved around the room. She failed the exam.

When you turn over the paper . . .

Be prepared to work hard

When you get into the exam room, be prepared to get your head down and work really HARD. It is only for a maximum of three hours or so anyway. Working hard here means thinking not just writing.

Read the exam paper very carefully

The first fifteen minutes of any exam are crucial. First read the bit at the top of the paper that tells you how many questions you have to answer and how much time you have. There shouldn't be any surprises here, but just check that it tallies with what you expected. Now read *all* the questions – carefully and at least twice. The second time is especially important because you tend to read too fast the first time and may miss the point. Make sure that you have read all the questions, including those over the page.

See which questions you could do

As you go through the second time, put little ticks against questions you think you could attempt. Jot down any ideas that immediately occur to you in connection with these questions, but don't just rush into the first question you think you can do, as there may be one further down the paper you could do even better. As you read down the paper you will be able to narrow your options. But don't chuck out questions as impossible without giving them a little thought. Are they really about some part of the syllabus you have neglected utterly? Or are they in fact about some very familiar subject that is just unfamiliar in presentation? Don't be thrown by the format of a question.

Look out for questions in two or more parts. It's no good doing a brilliant answer to Part One if you can't tackle Part Two at all. Watch out for indicators of how many marks a question is worth – exams will often list exactly how many marks are awarded for a question and this is very useful to know. If only one mark is on offer, there is no point giving a very detailed answer.

Choosing questions will be much easier for candidates with a poor knowledge of the syllabus, who will be able to pick out their more limited options very quickly. Better-prepared candidates may have more problems. Do not spend ages dithering between two questions that you could do equally well, or worse still, start one, then go back to the other, then think that the first one was a better bet . . . Disaster!

Should you do questions you have seen before?

If a question you have done before does come up on your exam paper, make sure that you think about your answer again – don't just write out your memory of what you did before, or it will sound stale. And make sure that you haven't forgotten anything vital. Be very careful with questions that are subtly different from the one you answered before – make sure you really answer the question on the paper and not the one you did in class.

Decide which questions you will do

Before you start any questions, decide which you will do. This means that you are making the important decisions while your mind is fresh. Later on, when you are more tired, you will only have the donkey work left to do.

Answer the right number of questions

If you answer too few you will lose marks needlessly, so try to get something down even if it is only a list of points. If you answer too many questions, the examiners will only take the best ones into account, or even the ones that come first, if they are really mean. Better for you to choose which *you* think would be the best ones for you to answer and then try to spend time working these ones up. Some further time spent thinking about a question can often improve your answer, even when you feel that you know nothing more about the subject – you may think of more ideas, or you may simply be able to tidy up your grammar or your logic. Remember to answer any compulsory questions – you must at least have a go at these.

Think about the questions

Once you have decided which ones to do, think hard about each question. What does it mean? You will get some marks for explaining in your introductory paragraph what you think the question calls for, even if you are then completely unable to supply this. Look at every question with a fresh eye. What is it really trying to get at?

Make plans

Always make a plan for an essay question. If you can possibly bear to, you should do plans for several of the questions before you start writing any of them up. This is tough advice to follow. There is all that valuable time ticking away and you haven't even started the first question. But in fact you will find that there are several advantages to this method:

- Your energy levels will be much higher at the start of the exam, so it will be easier to think straight.
- When you come to the end of the first question and you are a bit tired and behind on time, you can go straight into the second without having to psych yourself up into making a fresh plan: half your work will have already been done.
- Writing is easy if you have a plan. If you don't, it will sound disorganized and you will keep having to stop to get it back on track, which will be slow, and it may even peter out all together.
- When you come to the end of the exam, if you have no time to do the last question fully, you will at least have your plan. You will be able to write a quick list of points which you should get some credit for.
- Panic is the enemy of planning. As time gets short, you will panic more and plan less. So it makes sense to plan as much as possible near the start of the exam.

What to do if you are really stuck
If you are really stuck, look for questions which give you information. If a question is the sort where the paper supplies all the information and you have to demonstrate a skill using it, you are lucky.

EXAMPLES

Practical criticism on a literature paper
You will be asked to comment on a printed passage. This is a skill you probably either have or haven't got by this stage – you will know which. But at any rate, you don't need to have prepared specially for this sort of question so it is a good one to attempt. Be prepared to think hard in the exam, though, and to use the information given you to the best of your ability.

Document questions on history papers
The answers to these questions are often quite obvious from reading the source carefully, even if you know nothing about the historical facts. Look out for those questions which in fact demand a rather different skill than you would expect: for instance, questions on a history paper which ask you to analyse a lot of statistics, or read a graph. You may well find that quite a few of the marks go

for saying what the figures mean, which doesn't demand any historical knowledge at all, just common sense. And the figures may well jog your mind into remembering some historical facts: if they indicate that a lot of deaths occurred in Ireland in the 1840s, you might just remember that it was about then that the Potato Famine happened.

Look too for simple questions that demand a lot of organization. There will be a question on an elementary Maths paper, for example, that demands little more than a knowledge of basic arithmetic and a clear head to steer your way through a great deal of it.

Look for questions which ask for your ideas about a general statement, the sort of thing everyone has some opinion on. But remember to back up your opinion with facts. They needn't be facts you have learnt in class, but you do need evidence of some kind.

What to do if you don't recognize the questions at all

If you look through the exam and are totally thrown by all the questions – they are not what you expected at all – don't panic. This does occasionally happen: I went into one exam where we had been told that the questions would be more detailed questions on the set books, so we had all revised those thoroughly. In fact they were general questions on the nature of literature. But when we looked at the paper more closely, we found that we could answer the questions from the experience we had; it was a matter of thinking hard of what we could do *with* what we knew. Cut your losses – think of what you *can* do in the situation rather than what you *can't*.

When you are answering

Don't waffle

Try not to, however little you really know. It does put the examiner off. Remember that quality is more important than quality. Don't just write down every fact you know on the subject, however unrelated to the question – this is a real waste of time.

Watch your timing

Make a time plan. This is something you should work out before you get into the exam. You know how long you will have and how many questions, so work out how much time you should spend planning and making outlines, and how much time you should spend writing. This is up to you, and it will vary on how many questions you have, but a good guide is that 25 per cent of your time should be spent planning. So if you intend to be writing for an hour, spend fifteen minutes planning what you will say. Remember to leave time for planning the whole paper – reading the questions and deciding which ones to do – and for reading through your answers at the end, for a vital final check.

Look at your watch frequently to see how you are sticking to your time plan. Try not to get behind, and remember that you will gain more marks for the first paragraph of a new essay than the last paragraph of an old, however brilliant the latter may be. It is a terrible shame to ruin a good exam paper through not having time to do the last answer. However good your other questions are, you cannot do really well if you don't answer enough.

Ignore what is going on around you

Ignore what the other candidates are doing, they have nothing to do with you. Even if you think your friend is doing terribly well or badly, you will probably be wrong anyway. Concentrate on doing well yourself. Don't worry if everyone seems to be calling for more paper when you are on your first side – this is a well-known one-upmanship trick in exams. Remember that quality is far more important than quantity.

Remember the halo effect

A nicely presented paper, easy to read, with all your answers clearly set out, will immediately put the examiner on your side. Your answer paper will glow with virtue – it's called the halo effect. Is your handwriting legible? Ask an honest friend, and then see if he or she can read it when you are writing really fast. It is a good idea to practise writing at speed, to check that your hand doesn't get too sore and that your words are still clear. (Adrenalin may make you forget that your hand hurts, but it won't make your writing any clearer.) Readable handwriting will make it much, much easier for your examiner to give you marks. If you don't know how to spell a word in an exam, avoid it if possible, and certainly don't try and make it illegible to confuse the examiner. Examiners aren't that easily taken in!

Don't waste time by:

1. Writing out the question and underlining it in another colour. Just write out the number. The examiner will know what the question was.
2. Looking out of the window.
3. Feeling guilty about how little work you have done.
4. Feeling sorry for yourself.
5. Thinking about how other people seem to be doing.
6. Repeating yourself. Be especially careful not to repeat material from question to question either.
7. Writing full sentences when one word is called for.
8. Wishing that the questions were different.
9. Answering too many questions.
10. Writing little notes to the examiner. They will do you no good. Also avoid those artistic trailings off in the middle of sentences as if you have suddenly been shot at the end of the exam. To the examiner it makes no difference whether you have run out of time or didn't know the answer anyway – both are exam failings. Always finish your last sentence.
11. Daydreaming.
12. Panicking.
13. Cheating.

Part Two
Further Tactics

6

How to Study

When most people think about working for exams, they talk about 'revision'. 'I can't come out, I've got to revise,' is what they say to you. But just exactly what is revision? The dictionary defines it as 'to read or look over or re-examine or reconsider and correct, improve or amend'. All these words suggest going over something you have done already, 'seeing it again', in fact. But ideally, you should have the idea of the exam in your head long before you reach this final going-over stage. When you do the work for the first time, you should already be thinking about how you will have to use it later on in the exam room.

So this book talks not only about 'revision', but it talks about 'vision' as well, and the techniques of studying – the work that comes before revising, and the best way to do it in order to make revision easier. Bear the exam in mind throughout your course, however depressing this may seem at the time. It will bear fruit later.

Ideally, studying should involve learning new ideas and facts, and then applying them to new problems and situations. It should involve a questioning attitude: what am I getting out of this book, what have I learnt in this class? It shouldn't be a desperate attempt to memorize everything in sight. Unfortunately, because of exam pressure and lack of time, it sometimes seems as though it is. If you feel that your study is always like this, the next time you sit down with your books try to stand back and see the subject from a wider perspective. Allow yourself more time to understand things. Remember that passing exams is a by-product of studying, not its aim. And you will do better in your exams if you can put over the impression to the examiner that you like and understand the subject.

The three main ways of studying

There are three main ways of studying: in lectures or large classes where your teacher talks exclusively; in small classes or seminars where discussion is allowed; and through private reading. The techniques you will need vary for each one, so I will deal with each separately.

Lectures or large classes

Getting the most out of lectures can be very difficult. Sometimes the teacher's manner of presentation is so boring that you start day-dreaming and miss anything important that is said. At other times the lecture may be so packed with useful information that it is impossible to take it all in or get it all down on paper.

You need to think a bit about the lecture *before* you go to it. First, you need to decide whether to attend it at all (if this is an option). Is it relevant to what *you* have decided to study? Is the teacher usually good value? Make this decision in advance: don't decide to skip a lecture at the last minute because you are too lazy to go.

If you decide to go, you should think or read a little about the topic in advance. You will then understand what is being said more quickly and be able to pick up on special references and more advanced argument. You should get more out of the lecture this way. Decide what you want to learn from it, then if this doesn't figure, you could raise it in the question session at the end.

In the lecture, think about whether you want to take notes. Will they be useful? Sometimes it can be more helpful just to listen and then make a few private notes from memory afterwards. But if you feel that you need a concrete record to take away with you, bear the following points in mind.

1. It's going to be you who has to read them! So don't write so fast that your handwriting is illegible, make abbreviations that you won't be able to translate later, or cut down notes so much that they are incomprehensible.

2. Can you be bothered to write your notes out again? The world divides up into three sorts of people: those who spend ages sorting and rewriting their notes after each class; those who know that they won't have time, so make brief, neat notes to keep during the lecture; and those who always think that they will write them out

but never do. It's wonderful to be the first sort of person - writing out your notes should drive the facts into your minds. The second sort will have good notes to come back to when they do start revising. Don't be the third sort! Know yourself and be realistic about how much work you have time to do.

3. Think before you write. Listen for the main points of what is being said and try to get those down – don't aim for every little detail. Distinguish arguments and explanations from examples, and go for the arguments, with perhaps one example if you have time. Do your notes follow on logically? (Assuming the speaker is being logical, that is!)

4. If ideas occur to you while the talk is going on, jot them down too, but make sure you know afterwards whose ideas are whose. Put your initials against your own points if necessary. Don't get so carried away in your own thought that you miss what is going on.

5. Use plenty of headings, underlinings, numbered lists, colour (within reason!) and so on to make your notes easy to understand and pleasant to come back to. There is nothing so off-putting to revise from as undivided pages of scrawled handwriting.

□ *Think about what is being said, don't just try to get every word down*

Hand-outs

If you feel that your teacher goes too fast, you could always ask for a written hand-out with the main points on it. This may well be more accurate than your notes so is useful to have. But remember that unless you go through it yourself afterwards, making additional personal notes and underlining the main points, it won't be as good as your own notes for fixing what you have heard in your memory. It's writing things down and thinking about them as you do so that make you remember them. The more you can do this first time around, the less revision you will have to do before the exams.

What to do if you miss a lecture or class
Try to borrow notes from other people if possible, or get a teacher's hand-out. You should do this as soon as possible after the missed lecture, don't wait until you need the notes for revision. You may also need to borrow notes if you have daydreamed right through the class, which happens to all of us at some point. Try to get more than one set of notes from the same session if possible, as other

people may have their own peculiar and/or useless ways of note-making. Having two versions can also be a useful check to see that all the main points are there. You don't want to annoy your notemaking sources, so don't ask to borrow too often, or you may find your friends unwilling to lend you notes when you really need them.

Seminars or small classes

Seminars or small classes where you can discuss your reactions to a subject can be the most useful way of getting your ideas straight. Make the most of them. Even if you are shy, try to put forward contributions. If you are not shy, make sure that you are not hogging the conversation – listen to other people as well. They may well have useful things to say. Even if you feel they are putting something very badly, use the time constructively by thinking about how it could be said better. Beware of preparing your next comment while other people are talking; the conversation may well have moved on by then and you will be left in the lurch, as well as having missed what has been said in the meantime. Remember that seminar-type classes, together with your essays, give your teacher the main impression of what sort of student you are, so bear the hidden curriculum in mind (see p.63). Punctuality, politeness and interest will all make you seem a better student.

Don't forget that you can also make notes in seminars. It may be very handy to jot down the main ideas that come up, for later consideration.

Reading and private study

Although lectures can be interesting and informative and seminars a welcome break, you will probably do most of the real studying on your own. This is when being organized is really important, as you have to create your own schedules and disciplines. Keep lists and make timetables, ticking things off as they get done for a sense of achievement.

You may find that you seem to have an awful lot of reading to do and this can really make you panic, especially if you aren't that far off exams. Try and divide up this reading and classify it into different types as far as possible. Is it:

● *Essential* reading, such as your textbook, class notes or very important recommended reading, which you will need to read very carefully?

- *Additional* reading, which may have some very useful material in it, but needs to be read more selectively?
- *Wider* reading, for general interest, which may have some handy stuff in it, but is intended more to enlarge your feeling for the area?

Use different reading techniques to suit different types of material. There are three main ways of tackling your reading:

- *Skimming* through a book before you read it to see if it is worth reading, and if so, how carefully. Use the information on the contents page to see what is in the book, and read the description on the jacket, if it has one. Read a paragraph or two to see how difficult the style will be.
- *Reading at a normal speed*, taking notes where something interests you or seems useful to remember. When you come to an important passage, switch to
- *Reading slowly* to grasp a detailed argument, or to remember something that you will need. Check that you understand and go over the passage to help yourself to remember it. Take detailed notes. (Remember to switch back to normal speed once the material stops being so vital.)

It isn't as vital to read fast as to read selectively. You need to know what is important, and this means knowing why you are doing the reading. Use any help given you in the book to find your way around it. Signposts, such as 'The next section is about . . .' 'On the other hand . . .' 'To summarize . . .' will give you a guide to the structure. A diagram may present information more clearly than the text. Make sure that you can reproduce the main ideas of the book: analyse it briefly and write out the keypoints once you have finished.

Some people do find speed-reading techniques helpful, but check that you are still taking the material in at speed. It is always better to know fewer topics more thoroughly than to have a little information about a lot. In your exam you won't have time to write that much – it is the quality rather than the quantity that the examiners will be looking for.

How to cut down on your reading

If you seem to have a reading list that you can't possibly get through, cut it down. Make this decision yourself rather than having it made for you: decide what you will read and get it done, rather than conning yourself that you will be able to complete a huge list and then finding out at the last minute that you can't. Ask your teacher what is important. Ask other students what they found useful. Look out for books mentioned a lot in other books. And remember that you don't always have to read the whole book – a chapter may be sufficient.

Making notes while you are reading

It is very important to do this, as it will fix whatever you are learning in your mind. It is all too easy to drift off without noticing while you are reading – taking notes will keep you thinking. Much the same rules apply as for taking notes in class, but you will be able to set your own pace. Make sure you understand what you are writing down; if you don't, read it again before you write anything. If you still don't understand, make a note to ask someone about it. But don't go too slowly – you don't need to get everything down, and you certainly shouldn't be trying to write the whole book out again. Stick to the main points. If the book is wide-ranging in subject, make a note of where what you are reading fits in – and notice if it has changed.

Highlighter pens are handy if the book belongs to you (have mercy on Britain's library books), but remember that you will probably have to go through at some point writing out the points you have highlighted if you are to remember them properly, or if you want to slot them into your file.

Some ways of improving your study techniques

Studying is difficult. Working, disciplining yourself and learning new ideas is always going to be hard. If it weren't, it wouldn't be worth doing. Certainly some people do find some things easier than others, but all students, even those who are always top of the class, will come across problems and difficulties. The important thing is to find ways of dealing with the difficulty, to see a new way of looking at the problem, or to find the right person to ask, or the right book to read. Keep trying – think of things that caused you problems before but which you can do easily now. Often the most important thing is to find out exactly what is causing you the problem. It is this frame of mind which makes the good student, rather than the ability to solve every problem the first time around. Nobody knows automatically how to study – like every skill, it must be learnt. Notice when you make mistakes in studying – when you go about something the wrong way, for instance, or when you are disorganized and have to redo things and then try to avoid the same errors the next time. You will learn from your own mistakes, but here are some hints to bear in mind.

Get organized for study

Studying can seem incredibly daunting unless you are properly organized. Keep lists and timetables of assignments that must be completed and don't leave everything until the last minute. This is especially important if you have recently been given a lot more freedom to organize yourself – in the sixth form, for instance, or at college. It's all too tempting to enjoy your unexpected 'free' time, and then find yourself with a crisis on your hands. If you get behind with your work, you won't enjoy it or be able to do it well. Remember that you should also aim to do some work in the vacations. Don't attempt too much – that great pile of books can seem so depressing on holiday and you need a break – but try at least to get *something* done.

Keeping your notes well organized is psychologically important as well as timesaving. You will feel better about your work if you don't have to hunt through a huge pile of paper every time you want to find something. While you don't need to type all your notes into a personal computer database, or copy them on to card indexes (this is just whitening your tennis shoes, see p.17) it does help to have them in a recognizable order. Files and file dividers for subjects and subjects within subjects are useful. Loose-leaf files mean that you can add extra notes when necessary or replace old notes with an updated version. Cross-reference if necessary. (While this may sound complicated, in practice it need mean no more than writing 'See History of Ireland section' or whatever at the bottom of the page.)

Start organizing your notes early – there is nothing more dispiriting than a huge pile of unsorted paper at the start of a revision session. The other advantage is that you will be able to see early on which subjects you need to do more work on, and which you already have plenty of information about.

The hidden curriculum

Other things apart from your actual work can influence your teachers and lecturers, such as punctuality, politeness, interest in the subject and making an effort. It's always as well to bear this in mind: even if your exam paper is not marked by your teacher, he or she will be more willing to help you when necessary if you appear to be making an effort in general. If your teacher *is* marking your paper, these things are more vital than ever if you are to get good marks. If the possibility of getting the 'benefit of the doubt' crops up in marking your exam paper, you want an image of the keen and hardworking student to spring up immediately in your teacher's mind.

Using the library

Make the most of the resources available to you. Sometimes libraries can seem rather daunting places, but if you learn how the system works, they will be very useful to you. Most schools and colleges have introductory sessions at the beginning of term, but if you find that you still need help (and there is usually a lot of other information to take in at the beginning of term) the librarians will always be willing to help. Learn how to use microfiche directories and find out all the resources which your library has on offer – books, journals, newspapers, video tapes, cassette tapes, pictures, records. If you feel that your college library is limited, you may want to use a bigger one as well – see what your local town has to offer.

Using your friends

Talking to friends, in class or outside, can be a very useful way of learning new ideas and getting your own straightened out. It will also help you see that you are not the only one having difficulties. If you don't understand something, a friend may well be able to explain it; if you do, explaining it to them will help fix it in your own mind. Explaining something to another person is the greatest test of understanding. If you are having bigger problems – if your teacher doesn't seem to be following the syllabus, for instance – discuss the matter with your friends. It is better to approach your teacher as part of a group, so you don't just seem like a troublemaker.

Learn where things fit in

Always try to see the subject as a whole. This is particularly vital when taking exams, so that you can see which topics are important, but the earlier you can start to get an overview of a subject the better. It helps to have at least a vague idea of what the syllabus is expecting of you before you start the course. Ask yourself some more questions about what you are doing. Is the material that you are taking in an important new part of the syllabus? Is it a completely new topic, or is it part of something you have covered before? Is it a new skill, or another way of doing something you have done in a different way before? Does it consist of further examples of an argument you have already seen? Is it a vital part of the subject, or an interesting but not vital sideline?

In class, if you listen, you will get at the very least clues to these questions and probably complete answers. Remember to keep asking the questions! The teacher might say at the beginning of the lesson, 'Now we are looking at a new topic' or, 'These are some examples of what we did yesterday.' He or she might well say, 'This is very important for the exam'. Use these hints! If your teacher seems to be starting on a complete red herring, however – something completely irrelevant – have patience. It will probably become clear by the end of the lesson where he or she is heading. If it doesn't, ask.

If you are reading your textbook outside class, remember that it is probably pretty much geared to the syllabus you are taking. So the headings and chapter titles it uses will probably link up to those you are given in class. Use chapter headings and contents pages to help you find your way around books quickly and easily. If you are reading books that are outside the course – recommended additional reading, for instance – be aware before you start which area of the course they are connected with. Why did your teacher or whoever suggest that you read them? As you read, think of how things link up. For instance, if you heard one argument in class, does this one agree or is it the other side of the case? Is this instance an example of something you have already heard?

Keep asking yourself, 'Where does this fit in?' It may be in more than one place – in that case think about the new material in relation to both areas. Use this information in your notes, so you can take the right amount of notes *and* put them in the right place.

Understanding what you learn
Once you have decided where a subject fits into your course, the most important thing to do is to understand what you are told about it. Easy to say, but how can you make understanding easier for yourself?

☐ *The first step to understanding is noticing when you don't understand.*

Very obvious, maybe, but many people don't get that far. With some subjects it is easy to check when you don't understand. In Maths, for example, if you can't do the questions set on the topic you have just covered it is fairly clear that you need it explained again. But in others what 'understanding' means is less clear. Don't resort to memorizing when you don't understand. Try to think about why you have just been told something. Does it follow on from the last sentence you read or heard? Does it back up the argument or does it contradict it? One good test of understanding is to try to explain whatever it is to another person. Remembering things you understand is much easier than remembering those you don't. So try to understand the first time round rather than facing yourself with a set of confused notes when you come to revise. There's nothing that will make you panic quicker.

What to do if you don't understand
Break up the topic into the smallest possible units, and then try to pinpoint exactly where it is you stop understanding. If this doesn't in itself make you understand (and often it will – to read something again in this way can be a great help) it will make it much simpler for someone else to explain to you.

Don't be afraid to ask your teacher when you don't understand – that's what teachers are there for. If you feel that you will look a fool if you ask in class, go up after the session. Try asking friends or reading their work. Or try another source of explanation – your textbook, for instance, if you haven't understood the teacher.

Once you feel you have a vague understanding at any rate, try to do lots of questions on the subject. Or write out whatever it is from memory, or write an essay on it.

Remembering what you learn

The best way of remembering something is to understand it. But you may sometimes feel that you need extra help, especially at exam time, when you need to store away a lot of information. Try using the following memory aids or *mnemonics*.

The initials technique

This technique involves learning the initial letters of a set of facts. A list of letters, especially if grouped in a memorable way, can be much easier to remember than the real thing, and act as a quick prompt when you need to recall all the information.

So, for example, you might want to learn the Beatitudes in the Bible:

> *Blessed are the Poor in spirit; for theirs is the kingdom of heaven*
> *Blessed are they that Mourn; for they shall be comforted*
> *Blessed are the Meek; for they shall inherit the earth*
> *Blessed are they which do Hunger and thirst for righteousness; for they shall be filled*
> *Blessed are the Merciful; for they shall obtain mercy*
> *Blessed are the Pure in heart; for they shall see God*
> *Blessed are the Peacemakers; for they shall be called the children of God*

You could group these according to the letters capitalized above as follows: PMMHMPP, which makes 3P 3M H altogether, a combination which is quite easy to remember. This technique obviously relies on your knowing the information well enough for your brain to be triggered by the code. It's no good remembering 3P 3M H if you can't remember what it stands for. But it is a very good way of keeping information on the tip of your tongue short-term.

Photographic memorizing and learning by ear

You will know the ways in which your brain works – exploit them. If you can recall a fact by remembering its position on the page in your memory, use this talent by setting out your notes clearly so that you can see them in your mind. If you remember the sound of the words, say them to yourself often. Make facts into little rhymes or songs – it doesn't matter how silly they sound if it helps you to remember them. Think how many everyday pieces of information have been transformed into rhymes for this reason:

'I before E except after C.'

'Thirty days hath September, April, June and November.'
'A litre of water's a pint and three quarters.'

How are you doing?
Use the assessment system – your marks on pieces of work and exams, any conversations with your teachers – to tell yourself how you are doing and what you need to work harder at. You need to understand what is valued highly to score well, so notice what your teacher thinks is good and try to repeat it.

7

Essay Questions

Do not draw a skotch-map of the Battle of Bannockburn, but write not more than three lines on the advantages and disadvantages of the inductive historical method with special relation to ecclesiastical litigation in the earlier Lancastrian epochs.

'Know ye not Agincourt?' (Confess)

Exam paper from 1066 and All That

Essay questions are the most difficult of all to answer in exams. Not only do you have to know all the information, you also have to handle it well to argue your case, and all within less than an hour. These questions call for a lot of hard thinking and you should practise doing them in the time allowed.

Understanding the question

Perhaps the most important factor in answering any essay question well is understanding what it wants you to do. You must answer the question in front of you, and not just write down all you know about the subject. Essay questions are often set in a language all of their own – evaluate, diagnose and inwardly digest, they ask – and you will need to be able to translate this into your terms *before* you can begin. You will find a glossary of exam terms at the end of this chapter.

Making a start

First note all the key words in the question. Underline them and write down what you think they mean. As well as underlining key words for the subject itself, underline the words that show you how you should treat it. Take the following question, for instance, from an A-level English Literature paper:

□ *Consider in what ways* and *how effectively T.S. Eliot develops* the *theme of the nature of Christian martyrdom* in Murder in the Cathedral

'Consider' is just an exam word for 'write an essay on'. But in this question you are asked to consider both 'in what ways' and 'how effectively' the theme is used; in other words, you should describe and evaluate its use. Your own judgement is asked for. The word 'develops' is also important: what is entailed in developing a theme, and does T.S. Eliot do this? So you can see that there is more to this essay than simply writing on Christian martyrdom in *Murder in the Cathedral*.

Now write down any ideas that occur to you about the question. Think carefully about it, and try to recall any relevant classes you had or books you have read about it. If it is a question you haven't considered before, make sure you have thought about all the possible angles. If you are really stuck on the subject, try brainstorming, which is just writing down anything on the topic that occurs to you.

Making a plan
Next make a plan for how you will structure your argument. This is always essential if you are to present a clear argument, and particularly vital in exams when time is against you. The actual writing is also much easier if you have a clear idea of what you are going to say where. The stage where you think of ideas and the stage where you make a plan are interchangeable – a structure will probably begin to emerge as you think of ideas, and more ideas will come as soon as you have a structure.

Here is an example. Your question might be:
● 'Capital punishment is unjustifiable'. Discuss.

You could underline 'unjustifiable' and 'Discuss' here. 'Discuss' means it's an argument question. 'Unjustifiable' needs some more thinking about in your answer.

Make two columns, and then write down everything you can think of FOR the statement in one half and everything you can think of AGAINST it in the other. Here are two columns ready for you. You don't need to write a whole essay, but jot down a few ideas. Do this before reading on.

For Capital Punishment	**Against Capital Punishment**

(Your ideas might go something like this)

1. Criminals need punishment	5. Capital punishment is too severe
2. We must prevent crimes like murder from recurring	6. Criminals often don't repeat crimes
3. Capital punishment deters others	7. The possibilities of reforming criminals
4. The expense of prisons	8. All murder is wrong, including judicial murder

You will probably have thought of many more ideas, but these will do for a start.

It doesn't matter how strongly you feel about the subject, you must try to think of a few points on the other side, no matter how firmly you intend to knock them all down later. Imagine arguing with someone who really disagrees with you – what points would they come up with? Having a strong opinion is fine – you can probably tell from my plan that I am not in favour of capital punishment – but you must at least be able to put some points for the other side. Your exam paper will probably come up with rather controversial statements for you to discuss, so you shouldn't have too much trouble here.

Be careful of value judgements. My points 5 and 8 are, as they stand, my own opinion. 'Capital punishment is too severe'. Too severe for what? an examiner might say, or 'punishment can't be too severe'. I will need to make sure, when I make this point, that I back it up with some evidence, or that I make it quite clear that I know it is only an opinion: 'I feel that . . .' It is very useful, when you are doing an argument question, to have a sort of mental heckler present, pointing out all the flaws in your reasoning.

Now you have got the main points of your essay together, decide:

1. What you think
This may well have changed by the time you have put down all the fors and againsts. The advantage of deciding what you think first is that you won't change your mind in the middle of the question, which can have a disastrous effect on your argument.

2. How you are going to structure your essay

There are various ways of doing this. One approach is to write down all the points on one side, then all the points on the other, then come to a conclusion. This is sometimes known as the jury approach – you hear the prosecution and the defence and then make up your mind. This method has the advantage of being easy to organize. Its disadvantage is that you may sound as if you are saying things, then denying them several paragraphs later. If you are very strongly for or against the motion, you could get round this by putting all the points you disagreed with in a framework such as 'Opponents of this approach would argue . . .' and then knocking the arguments down later.

Another way of doing it is to discuss the pros and cons together. You might want to discuss a certain part of the argument where you came down strongly on one side, and then another where you didn't, and then come back to one where you did – possibly because these parts fit better together in this order, despite your conflicting opinions. The danger of this method is that it can lose all sense of structure, even though it may follow the actual patterns of logic better.

A third approach is to combine these two ways of structuring. Discuss points based on one side and then points based on the other. The difference from the first method is that you can go into arguments against the point as you discuss it, even though they strictly belong to the other camp, but your overall structure remains in place. I find this last method very successful. You need to start off with the arguments against the side you want to come down on, then you are likely to be more convincing. Although many of the marks are given for the act of arguing, you also want the examiner to agree with you.

Starting your essay

It is often a good idea to start your essay with a quick paragraph saying how you have defined the question. Then, even if the examiner does not agree with your definition, at least it is clear that you have made a decision and are sticking to it. In this opening paragraph, you could also briefly mention what you are going to cover, again giving a good impression that you know what you are talking about. This is also useful if you run out of time in your essay. One teacher of mine at school used to describe the ideal essay plan as 'say it, say it fully and say it again'. While I wouldn't go that far, it is a good idea to let the examiner know where you are going. Use signposts in your writing: 'On the other hand', 'However' and so on. Remember the signposts that were useful to you when *you* were reading and imitate them for your reader.

Value judgements and emotive words
Avoid using words that suggest you have already come to a conclusion until the end of your essay. For instance, don't say that 'capital punishment is wicked' without defining what you are using the word 'wicked' to mean. Your own opinions are important and there should be room in the question for you to show them, provided they are suitably backed up with examples, instances, and quotations. It is good to go into one example fully and then mention a few more in passing. (If you describe one fully and then just mention the others, it will look as if you can describe them fully too, even if you can't.) If you can't think of any evidence, try to work out why you started to hold your opinion in the first place – what convinced *you*?

Use of quotations
Don't make quotations too long. If there seems to be a lot of relevant evidence, you could paraphrase some of it (write it out in your own words) and then just quote the really essential bits. A page of quotation, however relevant, will look like time wasting and may really not leave you time to say anything about the quotation. Instead, show why you have chosen to use that particular one. Be careful of using the quotations that everyone always uses, unless you think you have really a new way of commenting on them. Quote accurately if at all possible. For some subjects this can be difficult – Shakespeare is a case in point – in which case you may be well advised to stick to paraphrase rather than producing very garbled versions of the original.

Using other people's opinions and crediting them
It is often very useful in an essay to quote someone else's ideas – it is unlikely that you will be able to come up with a whole essay full of new ideas on a topic – but always say if you are borrowing. If you firmly start your sentence, 'As so and so points out,' it will be clear that you are not trying to pass the idea off as your own and that you

are well-read. It is not necessary to do this with your own teacher's opinions, but check how much you agree with them before you write them out.

Arguing logically

Your arguments must follow on from each other. This is mainly a matter of structure, which you should have thought about *before* you started the essay, in your essay plan. If you have fresh ideas while you are writing, jot them down on rough paper and then see where they fit in. Don't just write them down – it is all too easy just to let your ideas carry you through the essay, and end up with a rather disorganized piece of thinking. This is an especial danger in exams, where the natural instinct is to get everything down as quickly as possible. Use paragraphs to help you keep to your structure. Each paragraph should have one main idea in it – and only one. The rest of the paragraph should be explaining this idea, or illustrating with examples. The next paragraph should follow on logically from the previous one.

Style

Everyone has their own individual style. But you should make sure that yours is in line with what is expected. Check whether it is acceptable to use 'I think' rather than a passive form like 'It would appear'. Don't use clichés. Style is an important contributor to the halo effect; if the way you write sounds intelligent and logical, the examiner will assume that you are too.

The enthusiasm factor

Teachers like to find people who are keen on their subject. Obviously you can't pass an exam just by emphasizing how much you enjoy Biochemistry, for instance, but an element of enthusiasm for the intrigues of an historical episode or the humour of a novel can get you a long way. Make your essay sound as if you enjoyed writing it.

Waffling

Don't waffle just to fill space. It is better to be brief and coherent on what you do know than vague and lengthy on what you don't. If you know absolutely nothing about the subject it is better to spend more time on another question than to write rubbish. Don't repeat yourself needlessly to fill space either. There is nothing more off-putting to an examiner than an essay which doesn't know where it is going. Keep thinking 'Is this relevant?'. 'Does this fit in?'. Waffling will make your halo slip faster than anything else.

Put yourself in the reader's shoes

Keep thinking, as you write, of the person who will be reading your essay. What will they want to know next? What questions might they be asking? Does what you have just written make sense, and if not, how should you make it clearer? Is there an example you can give of this fact? Summon up the bystander again – this time he is on your side, but he needs things clearly explained. There is no need to patronize the reader – don't use phrases like 'you see' (just think of some politicians and you should know what to avoid) – but you should make your essays easy to read.

Check your work

Make sure that you go through what you have written after you have finished, checking for spelling mistakes and anything that isn't clear. Check that your essay follows on logically. Also look out for slips of the pen – such as writing 'orgasm' throughout for 'organism' (it does happen') – and for words which are easily confused such as 'affect' and 'effect', 'your' and 'you're' or 'its' and 'it's'. Rewrite any illegible words – you want your essay to be as easily understood as possible.

Glossary

Here are some terms that are often used in exam questions. Make sure that you know what they all mean. Understanding an exam question is usually half the battle. You need to be able to cut through the words of the question to the meaning below. If you know what the question really means, you will write with greater clarity and confidence and will structure your answer correctly. This will impress your examiner.

If strange words crop up in your practice exam questions and they aren't on this list, do ask your teacher. Then write down the word and its definition at the bottom of this glossary and learn it along with the rest.

Agree
Don't just say yes or no, but show why, or why not.

Argue
Not what you do with your friends, but argue a case, take sides.

Analyse
Examine thoroughly, divide something into all its component parts.

Assess
Show how much you think something is worth, and say why. Weigh up points for and against, strengths and weaknesses and state your conclusion clearly.

Comment on
Describe and then give your own opinion.

Compare
Show the similarities and differences between two things.

Compare and contrast
Much the same as 'compare' or 'contrast' singly – show the similarities and differences between two things.

Consider
Think about in words, describe. This word will usually be followed by a word like 'discuss' or 'analyse'.

Construct
Make – usually used for a table or a diagram.

Contrast
Show the differences between (which usually entails pointing out the similarities as well).

Criticize
Talk about a subject and say what you think of it – which needn't necessarily be destructive. Present a balanced argument showing both positive and negative points.

Define
Either a straight dictionary meaning, or, more likely, a wider discussion of what something means.

Describe
As it suggests – give a description of.

Discuss
Argue the rights and wrongs of a subject.

Distinguish between
Show the differences between.

Evaluate
Say what something is worth or how important it is, citing the advantages and disadvantages, evidence for and against, etc.

Explain
As it suggests, say why, giving your own opinion if the question seems suitable.

Factors
Circumstances, facts or influences contributing to a result.

Give an account of
Describe.

Give reasons for
Exactly what it suggests – say why something is so.

How did . . .
A straight factual description is called for.

How far do you . . .
How much would you go along with a statement; asking for a personal opinion.

How would you . . .
Asking for a personal response.

Identify
As in 'identify the factors' – show what they are.

Interpret
Come to some conclusions from the evidence.

Justify
Show that a statement is right or true, giving evidence to support your views.

Learn from
As in 'what do we learn from' – what does it tell us?

List
As it suggests – make a list of. Be wary of slipping out of sentence forms, though, unless you are sure that it is allowed.

Name
As it suggests, although more than just a name may well be called for.

Note
Describe briefly how.

Outline
Give a brief description of.

Refer to
Asking you to use a particular source or book or argument. Make sure that you do.

Review
Go over and give a description of. 'Review in the light of X' – discuss, taking X into account.

Say whether you feel
Give your personal opinion, backed up by facts.

Show how
Describe the events leading up to, or the reasons for.

State
Present the main points simply and clearly.

Suggest
As in 'suggest why' – give possible reasons.

Summarize
Give a brief outline of.

Support
Use the diagram/document to support your answer – back up what you say with evidence from other material.

To what extent is
Usually, 'how far do you agree with the statement'.

Trace
Describe the events chronologically in narrative form.

What do you understand by . . .
Define.

8
Maths and Science Questions

A lot of people find maths and science exams the most frightening of all, perhaps because they offer least opportunity for improvisation. But even if you haven't a natural talent for these subjects you can do all right if you don't panic and stay organized.

The main things to remember are:

- Recognise which skill is being tested
  Don't just plunge into a question in the hope that you might be able to do it. Work out first what sort of question it is. Then you will be better prepared to do it – or able to find another one if it is something you haven't practised enough.
- Explain to the examiner what you are doing
  Make everything clear, by using words to explain when figures are not enough, providing diagrams where these are useful, and by showing every single step in your reasoning. Remember that marks are given for your working, not just for the answer.
- Don't panic
  Because of the nature of maths and science usually, you can either do a question or you can't – students are more likely to panic in these exams. Don't. Panicking in these exams is especially dangerous – there is nothing more likely to stop you thinking clearly. Get as far as you can with each question, making sure each step makes sense logically. Then think hard about the remainder. Remember that if you put down the right answers you have to get the marks: it isn't a question of an examiner's opinion.
- Get your timing right
  Make sure that you don't spend too long thinking about a hard question so you have no time to do an easy one. Structure your

time before you start and do the questions you feel most confident about first.

- Lay everything out neatly
  Presentation is especially important in maths and science exams. Space your work clearly, writing on every other line when using lined paper, so that it is immediately obvious what you are doing, and make sure your handwriting is legible.

The following example shows how you should tackle a maths question.

The question:

Parvinda's dad runs Tali's Take-away. He buys his rice from Yaul's Cash and Carry. A 45 kg bag costs £28.50. He uses 150 g rice for a portion.

(a) How many complete portions will he get from one bag?

(b) How much does the rice for one portion cost to the nearest penny?

The foil tray he puts the rice in when he sells it cost £17.60 + VAT for 2000. VAT is 15%.

(c) How much does it cost Parvinda's dad to sell 1 portion of rice? He charges 35p for a portion of rice.

(d) What is the cost to Parvinda's dad of the rice and container as a percentage of the selling price?

Parvinda's dad fixes all his prices so that the basic cost of the food and container is the same percentage of the selling price as the rice. His weekly expenses are:

    Rent £34.00   Water rates £12.50   Rates £23.00   Gas £49.00
    Electricity £19.60

(e) One week he takes £407.50. How much profit does he make?

How to set out your answer:

a) A 45 kg bag of rice costs   £28·50

   one portion of rice cost = 150g

   number of portions in a bag = 45kg/150g

                                = 4500/150g

                                  = 300

b) 300 portions cost £28·50

   1 portion costs £28·50/300 = £0·095

   TO THE NEAREST 1p. = 10p

c) 2000 foil trays cost £17·60 plus vat at 15%

   £17·60 + VAT at 15% = £17·60 × 1·15 = £20·24

   ∴ 2000 FOIL TRAYS COST £20·24

   ∴ 1 FOIL TRAY COSTS   £20·24/2000

                        = £0·0101

                        = 1p to nearest p.

Total cost of one portion of rice

plus foil tray = 11p

d) He charges 35p for 1 portion of rice

   11p as % of 35p = $\frac{11}{35}$ × 100 = 31·4%

   Cost = 31·4% of selling price

e) Weekly expenses :

rent	34·00
water	12·50
rates	23·00
gas	49·00
electricity	19·60
Total =	£138·10

He takes £407·50

$$\text{Cost of food and trays} = 31.4\% \text{ of } £407.50$$
$$= 0.314 \times £407.50$$
$$= £127.95$$
$$\text{Profit} = £407.50 - £127.95 - £138.10$$
$$= £141.45$$

General points about maths and science exams

Many mathematics and science exams are arranged so that each paper consists of two parts. Part A is made up of short questions which test basic skills; Part B has longer questions which test your ability to apply these skills in more complex situations. To take a simple example, a Part A question in mathematics might ask you to solve a quadratic equation, while a Part B question might ask you to solve a problem about velocity, time and distance which leads to a quadratic equation which then has to be solved. Is your paper like this? Check. In some exams, these parts may consist of different papers, but the basic idea is the same.

If your exam seems to be divided up in this way, a sensible strategy is to practise all of the Part A material as much as possible, using past papers, but to be more selective about Part B. If you have only a limited time for revision and are not too confident about your grasp of the subject, then it is best to devote about 75 per cent of your time to Part A and 25 per cent to Part B. The range of topics covered in B is not that wide and you should choose perhaps three or four topics to concentrate on and ignore the others. Remember that all Part B questions require Part A skills and unless you have a good grasp of these you won't be able to tackle Part B properly either.

Some general hints about revising for Part A

Get down to trying past papers straight away. Each question will be looking for a particular skill. As you try the questions in your past papers, make a note of what skill is being tested. For example, a question in Physics might test your ability to apply the basic rule:

☐ Heat required = Mass (Kg) x Change in temperature (K) x Specific heat capacity (J/kg K)

Call this equation 'specific heat capacity' and note whenever it occurs. It won't always be in the same form – you will need to look out for the different ways in which it may crop up. Another question on the paper might probe into how this rule is extended to take account of what happens when a substance changes state from liquid to gas. Some heat is required to effect the change of state from liquid to gas, but the temperature of the gas immediately after the change is the same as the temperature of the liquid just before. This is called latent heat capacity, so make a note 'latent heat' and so on. After a while you will recognize the skill the question is after quite quickly, and you can test yourself to make sure you have it at your fingertips.

Making this list of skills is important because without it you could get the impression that there is no end to the things which could be asked. This is not true. The list of skills required is quite short, and it is very comforting to get to the stage where you keep recognizing skills which you have already noted rather than making a note of new ones.

☐ *Making a list is the first step in being able to recognize which skill is being tested.*

When you try the past papers, don't flit from one to another. Try to work through the Part As in a methodical way. If you cannot do a question then find out how to do it by looking at a textbook or study guide. Ask a friend, or your teacher. This is the most important moment in your revision – you have found a weak point or a patch of ignorance, and now you have to do something about it. If you succeed, and overcome the difficulty, then you are well on your way to success. So you must overcome it. This is coming to the crunch.

☐ *The crunch: a simple Part A question you have no idea how to answer.*

The point of starting straight away on past papers is to bring you to this crunch point as soon as possible. It is quite common for students to revise by reading their notes and examples without ever trying questions. They are afraid of finding out that they can't do them. They then find this out during the exam when it is too late to do anything about it. To avoid this happening to you, be strong and try to complete each Part A question before moving on to the next. Don't make the mistake of trying Part B at this stage. You need to develop your muscles before doing this.

Some hints on how to answer Part A questions

A Part A question will be asking you to recognize which skill is being tested and to display that you have got it. Nothing else. If you cannot recognize what is required don't fudge or guess. This never works and wastes your valuable exam time. Worse, writing something which is obviously wrong (fudging) gives the examiner the impression that you are totally ignorant of the subject and this is a bad thing to do. You want to show that you have the subject under control – it's the halo effect at work again.

☐ *Never fudge or guess*

Once you have spotted which skill is being tested, set about demonstrating that you have it. Don't forget to put in a few words explaining to the examiner what you are doing. Students often see the examiner as someone who possesses infinite knowledge so, quite reasonably, they feel no need to explain what they are doing. It is better to see the examiner as an intelligent but ignorant person who needs things to be explained.

In science questions you should always put in the units. You might have the following question to answer:

☐ Question 1. Calculate the heat required to raise the temperature of 100g of copper by 5° C (the specific heat capacity of copper is 400J/Kg K).

You should write down:

☐ Specific heat capacity of copper = 400J/Kg K
Mass = 100g = 0.1 kg
Increase in temperature = 5° C = 5° K

Heat required = 0.1kg x 5° K x 400 J/Kg K = 200J

The way *not* to answer the question is to write down:

Heat = 100 x 5 x 400 = 200 000

This is meaningless (and wrong if the answer should be in
    joules).

The extra trouble needed to write down the units may seem like a
waste of time but it is good insurance against silly mistakes – for
instance, failing to notice that the mass is in grams while the specific
heat capacity is per kilogram.

In questions which test mechanical mathematical skills, words
can seem unnecessary. For instance consider the following very
simple question:

□ Question 2. Solve the equation $17x - 1 = 2x + 29$.

The steps, in full, are as follows:

$17x = 2x + 30$ (adding 1 to both sides)
$15x = 30$ (subtracting 2x from both sides)
$x = 2$ (dividing both sides by 15)

I have put the words which describe the steps in brackets, but when
you take the trouble to write down the separate steps, as above, the
words are not necessary. The actions speak for themselves. But if
this is to be so, the steps in the algebra must be clearly set out, and
not jumbled up as in this attempt at the question:

$17x - 2x - 1 = 15x = 29 + 1 = 2$

This way of writing down the solution is all too common. Notice
that most of these 'equals' statements are not even true. For
instance, $17x - 2x - 1$ is not equal to 15x and $29 + 1$ is not equal to
2. In this solution the student has fallen into the trap of using = as
punctuation and has forgotten its true meaning. The only cure for
bad habits of this sort is to go back, for a while, to writing in the
words which describe what you are doing, as I did in the brackets
above.

In other sorts of maths questions, such as arithmetic in daily life, words are an essential part of both the method and the answer. Here is an example of this sort of question:

Question 3. If the exchange rate is 10.68 French francs to the £1 and commission is charged at 1%, find the cost of purchasing 1000 French francs.

The best way of answering this is to imagine you are preparing a receipt for a customer, in such detail that he or she can easily check that the price charged is correct.

Exchange rate FFr 10.68 = £1
1 FFr = £1/10.68 = £0.093632
1000 FFr = 1000 x £0.093632 = £93.6329
Commission @ 1% = £0.93634
Total cost of 1000 FFr = £94.56924 = £94.57 to two decimal places

This question is testing whether you can get the right answer *and* whether you can show clearly how you got it.

Using your calculator
If you are studying maths or science your calculator is enormously important to you. Get familiar with its workings; experiment with it. The golden rule is always to have a rough idea of what the answer to a calculation should be, so that if you press the wrong buttons, or the right buttons in the wrong order, you will spot your mistake. If you have a long calculation to do, don't tie yourself in knots to avoid writing down anything but the final result. Break the calculation into smaller parts and write down the result of each part. All calculations should be checked, but it is particularly important with long ones where you could easily have made a mistake. Checking is much easier if you can check each part separately.

Some maths exams forbid the use of calculators in multiple choice or Part A. This is to test whether you understand the basics of arithmetic. If this is the case with your exam you should try to do the questions without using a calculator when you are revising but then you should check your answers with a calculator to see that you are right. If you were wrong then use the calculator to see why you made the mistake by tracking through your working. For example, the question might have asked you to express the answer to

$$1/2 + 1/3 — 1/4$$

as a single fraction in its simplest form. The steps in doing this are first to find a number which is exactly divisible by 2, 3 and 4. The answer is 12. Then each fraction must be expressed as something over 12 giving

$$6/12 + 4/12 — 3/12$$

which is 7/12. The answer to the question can be checked using the fractions button on your calculator, and if you got it wrong then each of the steps which you went through to get your answer can be checked on the calculator, so you can track down exactly where you went wrong. So don't think that because calculators are banned from Part A you should make no use of them during your revision. Practise doing the questions without calculators but use them to see where you go wrong and to put you right.

The proper use of calculators is now universally accepted as an important part of mathematical training, but initially many people felt that to depend too much on calculators was a bad thing. In fact calculators offer people the opportunity to learn far more about mathematics than they possibly could without, so the chances are that the more you use your calculator the better you will be at doing arithmetic without it.

Drawing diagrams and graphs
In science questions, diagrams can be very helpful to make what you are saying clearer. But they will only help your answer if they are neat and well labelled. A good diagram should show the information at a glance. In an exam, when you are in a hurry, you will only get one go at drawing your diagram – you don't have time for false starts and rethinking your layout. The answer is to give yourself plenty of room – at least half a page, and more if the diagram is to be complex. Draw diagrams in pencil, so you can rub out any mistakes neatly, and label them clearly in ink. Don't be tempted by diagram stencils, even if you can't draw a retort, because they are usually too small to be of much use to you. Useful

equipment consists of a sharp pencil, a good rubber, and a ruler; a coin can be useful for drawing small circles, and a plastic flexicurve will be helpful if you are doing graphs. Don't use colour and remember the conventions of each subject – for instance, that heat is shown by an arrow rather than drawing a flame. When you are drawing graphs, remember to label the axes, and check *before* you start that your graph will fit on to the paper in the scale you have chosen. In general, don't just draw diagrams for the sake of drawing them, even if they are ones you have learnt. Only include them if you feel that they will help your answer.

In some diagrams detail is important. In figure 1, for example, all the details are necessary. Look what happens in figure 2, which looks almost the same, *but*

(a) there is no rubber bung on the flask, so the carbon dioxide could escape through the top of the flask,

(b) the thistle funnel, used for adding the hydrochloric acid, does not go down below the level of hydrochloric acid in the flask so carbon dioxide could escape up the thistle funnel, after the hydrochloric acid is added,

(c) the test tube used to collect the carbon dioxide looks as though it has simply been placed over the end of the tube from the flask without first evacuating all the air. In figure 1 the level of water in the test tube is higher than the level in the dish indicating that the test tube was initially full of water.

Notice that there is no need to label the flask, thistle funnel, dish, test tube etc. The important thing is to make sure that your figure makes clear what each piece of apparatus is doing. If you don't think this is clear from your diagram, add a label to make it clear. For example, the thistle on the thistle funnel should make it clear that the dilute hydrochloric acid is poured down the funnel onto the marble chips, but to play safe you might feel like adding a label: 'hydrochloric acid poured in here'.

The point of some diagrams is to draw attention to the main point of an argument or description without lumbering it with too much detail. Figure 3, for example, displays the nitrogen cycle in the simplest form. The point the figure is making is that it is a cycle, involving plants, animals and soil. All the detail is added in the description. Don't be tempted to add detail to your diagram, as in figure 4. However much you enjoy drawing cows, resist the temptation. All that matters is the cycle.

Figure 1

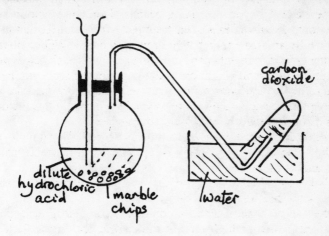

Figure 2

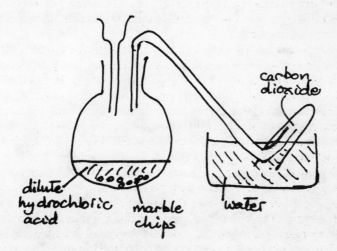

Figure 3

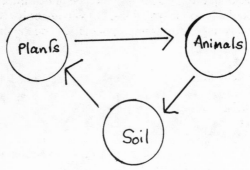

The Nitrogen Cycle

1. Plants take up nitrogen from soil.

2. Animals eat plants.

3. Animals excrete, die and decay,
   which returns nitrogen to the soil.

Figure 4

Some hints about Part B questions

You are now feeling quite comfortable about Part A and are ready to tackle Part B. First take your past papers and look through all the Part Bs. Don't try to do the questions at this stage. The object is to see what types of question come up. It can be quite difficult to spot the type if you don't do the questions, but you are only after rough categories at this stage. For example, in maths, you might spot the following types:

arithmetic in daily life
geometry
graphs – drawing
using statistics

In your list there will be some topics that you should decide to concentrate on. Don't spread yourself too thinly – you won't be able to revise the whole syllabus thoroughly. Choose a few types of question to work at. Now go back to your books and notes and refresh your mind about only those topics. Don't spend too long on this, but it is worth seeing what is involved before you start the past papers. Part B questions are longer and more difficult than Part A, and you need to have revised the bare bones of the topic before you can usefully tackle them.

Once you start trying the past papers, the first skill you need to develop is to recognize 'your' questions – the ones which belong to the groups you have chosen to concentrate on. Go through several years of papers and mark the ones you will try with some handy shorthand such as G for graphs, S for statistics and so on. Then go through and try all the ones marked G. There may be a few surprises – questions can turn out to be about something different once you get down to doing them, but you will learn something about recognizing questions from these experiences.

As you go through all the questions of a particular type you will build up skills and knowledge but you will probably need to return frequently to your books and notes in the process. If one question really defeats you then set it to one side and continue with the others, but don't move to another topic until you are really confident about the one you are working on. It is a good idea to write out answers carefully and neatly at this stage and to keep them for future reference.

9

Multiple Choice Questions

Multiple choice questions are those which give you a number of alternative answers and ask you to pick the right one. In some exams you make your choice by putting a tick in the box next to the alternative you want to select; in others you have to make the mark on a special answer sheet. As there is little or no writing involved you can answer many more such questions in an hour than you could conventional questions, so they make it possible to test a very wide range of topics. Each separate question is quite simple but together they aim to test your basic knowledge of the whole subject. Some exam papers will ask you to answer multiple choice questions along with other sorts of question. Others consist of nothing but multiple choice. This chapter will put forward a general strategy on how to do a whole multiple choice paper, but if you have just a few of these questions, read the chapter anyway for tips on how to answer individual questions.

Many people find the multiple choice paper in an exam the most off-putting of all. There are several reasons for this. One is that an answer must be right or wrong – there are no near misses or good tries. Another is that the rules for filling out special answer sheets must be followed to the letter, and a slip can be disastrous, but by far the most common reason is that the questions must be answered quickly because there are so many of them, and the very thought of this puts some people into a panic.

☐ *The important thing to realize is that multiple choice questions are different and that they call for different exam techniques.*

As you revise for multiple choice, bear in mind the sorts of question you are going to be asked. They will probably be fairly straightforward factual questions – have a look at your past papers to check – so you should concentrate on learning the key points about each topic. Avoid the trap of thinking that the multiple choice papers are easy and don't need much revision because you don't have to write anything. In fact you need to have the subject at your fingertips to answer questions fast and this calls for thorough preparation. Just think of *Mastermind*! Past papers are very useful to test yourself with; although the examiners are unlikely to ask the same questions from year to year, you will be able to see which topics you are still shaky on.

Once you are fairly well into your revision you will want to practice doing a complete paper to time. Here is the strategy you should try to employ:

A general strategy for multiple choice papers

In summary, the strategy is to start at the beginning and to work steadily through to the end, without spending too long on questions you can't immediately answer.

Read each question carefully, and don't look immediately at the list of alternatives. Multiple choice questions tend to divide up into two types: those which require you to know a fact, and those which want you to work something out. Which sort is the question you are looking at? If it is the first type, you will probably know immediately if you know the right answer or not. If you think you do, look down the list to see if your answer is there. If it is, you are home and dry – make the right mark and move on to the next question.

Beware of the idiot's answer. There is always one alternative waiting to trap the dozy candidate who is half asleep and not really thinking. When you have made your choice, take a moment to check that you have not fallen into this trap. It helps if you practise identifying the idiot's answer as well as the correct one when you do questions for revision.

If the question is the second type and wants you to work something out, ask yourself whether you know how to do this. For instance, if you are asked to solve an equation, do you know the correct procedure? If you do, work through the question quickly and check whether your answer tallies with one of the alternatives. If it doesn't check through very quickly to see that you haven't made an obvious mistake, but don't spend too long on this.

If you don't immediately know the answer or how to work it out, or if your working doesn't come up with a possible answer, do not spend more than two minutes thinking about it. If you cannot come up with the answer in this time you probably won't be able to at all. Rather than wasting time on questions you can't do – and which will only carry one mark – move on to ones that you may be able to do. This doesn't mean that you should rush through the paper in a panic, convincing yourself that you can't do any of the questions. But if you have thought *carefully* about a question for two minutes and still can't do it, you should cut your losses and move on. There may be easier plums for picking later on and you don't want to miss them.

Before you abandon the question, however, have a guess at the answer, UNLESS YOUR EXAM PAPER WILL PENALIZE YOU FOR GIVING THE WRONG ANSWER. If this is the case, don't guess – you don't want to lose marks. But most multiple choice exams will give you one mark for the correct answer, and no marks for an incorrect one. This means that if you don't know the answer to a question you should guess it. If there are five alternatives your chance of guessing the right one is 1/5.

Don't think that you can leave everything up to your lucky stars though. When the number of questions is large, the chance of your guessing the right answer even half the time is very low indeed. To improve your chances, try to eliminate some of the alternatives. You may well be able to get rid of at least one – the idiot's answer, perhaps.

When you have made your guess, don't actually make a mark in the box or on the answer sheet. Instead, use a code in the margin, well away from the boxes, and indicate those questions you have guessed. When you reach the end of the paper, come back to these questions. If you have time, think about them a little more and see if you can come up with the right answer or at least a more educated guess. If you are pushed for time, just mark your original guess on the answer sheet or in the box.

Be very careful with answer sheets. They are often marked by computer, so you need to read the instructions carefully and make your pencil marks absolutely clear. If you leave spaces to come back for guesses, make sure that you are still on the right number – you don't want to get one out and ruin all your answers.

As in any exam, don't cheat. It may seem very tempting,

especially in exam rooms where everyone is very close together and you can see the pattern of your clever friend's answers. But do try to resist temptation – the invigilator will be especially wary of cheating in multiple choice, and you are likely to get caught. Some multiple choice exams are deliberately set in varying forms – your neighbour may be answering the paper the opposite way round. You may not be able to see as clearly as you think, either, and get all the answers one place to the other side – a foolproof method of doing really badly. And who's to say that the person you are copying from is doing that much better than you are? Your chances are better if you stick to doing the paper yourself.

Some examples of multiple choice questions
From Modern History
Following a picture of a refugee camp in East Jordan during the 1960s, a question asked where the Arabs in the picture were most likely to have come from:
(a) Iran
(b) Lebanon
(c) Saudi Arabia
(d) Palestine
(e) Iraq
The idiot's answer is Saudi Arabia, which might be chosen simply because it has the word Arab in it. The correct alternative is Palestine. The others seem plausible because they have all been in the news recently.

From Maths
The sum of 1/5 and 3/4 is:
(a) 3/20
(b) 4/20
(c) 4/9
(d) 16/20
(e) 19/20
The idiot's answer is 4/9, obtained by adding the tops and bottoms of the two fractions and putting one over the other. Two others, (a) and (b), can be eliminated because they are less than 3/4. So if you really cannot add two fractions the answer can be narrowed down to a choice between two alternatives. On the other hand, if you can, then the answer is $4/20 + 15/20 = 19/20$.

Another one from Maths

A man bought some wood and was charged £18 plus VAT at 15%. His total bill was

(a) £2.70
(b) £18.15
(c) £19.20
(d) £20.70
(e) £33.00

The VAT on £18 at 15% is 2.70 and this is the idiot's answer, specially designed for someone who has not read the question carefully and has therefore missed the fact that it asks for the total bill. Alternative (b) is meant for the candidate who does not notice the % sign on the 15. Unlike most exams, multiple choices are often trying to lure you into making common errors, so be warned!

10

GCSE and Coursework

What is GCSE?
The initials GCSE stand for General Certificate of Secondary Education. This is the new examination recently introduced by the Government to replace the old GCE O-Levels and CSEs.

Why was it introduced?
It was felt that a fairer examination system was needed – one that would test a wider range of students more efficiently and not introduce an unnatural split at the age of sixteen, with some students taking O-Levels and others CSE.

How do the new GCSEs correspond to O-Levels and CSEs?

CSE	GCSE	GCE O-level
	A	A
1	B	B
	C	C
2	D	D
3	E	E
4	F	
5	G	

You can see by looking at this table how the new grades correspond to the old O-level and CSE grades.

What is different about GCSE?

There is more emphasis on what you can do as opposed to what you can't in GCSE – you will find questions at all levels to suit different people. So it is easier to show what you are good at.

In some subjects you can choose which papers you take – with corresponding effects on the grades you can achieve – in order to prevent students having to take papers where they have no hope of being able to answer the questions. Do you know which papers you have to do to get the grades you want in your subjects? If you don't, find out *now*. Don't leave it till the last minute. In GCSE French, for example, you can take various combinations of the following tests:

Basic Speaking
Higher Speaking
Basic Listening
Higher Listening
Basic Reading
Higher Reading
Basic Writing
Higher Writing
(These tests, and the names given them, may vary from board to board, but the main idea is the same)

Basic Speaking, Basic Listening and Basic Reading are compulsory tests – everyone has to take them. But if you *only* do these three, the highest grade you can get is E, however well you do in them. To get a maximum grade D, you have to do another test as well – you can choose which one. To get a maximum grade C, you have to add Basic Writing to this. For a B you must add Higher Writing as well. And if you want to get an A you must do another of the Higher tests on top of this.

You can see that you need to be very clear about which tests you are doing. Remember that doing the required tests doesn't guarantee you the grade, but not doing them does mean that you *won't* get it. On the whole, it is safer to do more papers than the minimum – that way you have a better chance. Ask your teacher for advice on what you should attempt.   On the whole GCSE questions are designed to be more practical and to have more relation to real life than those in the old exams: many of them will produce real situations and ask you to comment or act upon them. History papers include photographs and political cartoons for comment; business studies exams will ask you to analyse real case studies. The emphasis is on practicality.

A large amount of coursework is introduced into the syllabuses of most GCSE exams, with some exceptions such as French. Because of this, I have included a section on how to cope with coursework (pp. 97-107), although it is not, strictly speaking, an examination problem. But even if you are not taking GCSEs, you will want to do well in your coursework as it is useful for you to revise from and gives your teachers a good impression of your capabilities.

The advantages of being tested on coursework

The GCSE examiners feel, to use exam language, that coursework is able to test you on 'a greater range of skills'. That means that you have more opportunity to show what you are good at. You can show different sorts of achievement – larger projects which need more time than is possible in an exam; or an assignment which shows that you can gather information from a wider variety of sources; or work of a more practical kind. You will probably have some say in choosing what you do, rather than being given a fixed set of questions to answer.

You will also be able to show your social skills: you may well be set projects which test how well you can communicate with others, or your ability to work in a group.

You have the possibility of developing your work – of discussing it with your teacher and altering and improving it before you hand it in. And your work will be marked by someone who knows you well.

But perhaps the greatest advantage of having a coursework component is that you don't have to prove yourself in a short time under special and stressful circumstances, when you may or may not be feeling your best. GCSE aims to be more like normal class assessment than traditional exams. After all, if you are assessed in one way for the two years leading up to an exam, why should you suddenly be assessed in a very different way for the mark which really matters?

However, many of the same talents are needed for continually assessed courses as for traditional exams.

Know the exam

It is vital to know what *sort* of work you are going to be required to do, then you can decide how best to prepare for it. Coursework and exam work call for two different sorts of preparation. You should be aware of the percentage of marks awarded for exam and coursework components. If your coursework carries a high proportion of the marks, this is a clear sign that the examiners put emphasis on it. So you should too! If the coursework carries a low percentage, however, don't ignore it, but aim to give more of your time to preparing for the exam. Once you know how much coursework you will be required to do, find out what *sorts* of work are required, so you can prepare well for each. You will probably have a variety of different projects to complete.

Plan your campaign

Make a list of your assignments for each subject you are taking, including approximately how long you think they will take to complete, and when they are due to be in by. Make sure you know when the deadlines for your coursework are – if you don't, the chances are you won't get them in on time. Check! Now make a timetable of course assignments. If too many deadlines seem to appear in the same week, tell your teachers – they will probably be able to shift the dates around to make it easier for you. If you seem to have an impossible amount to do, ask for help! As long as you point out well in advance how many assignments you have due that week, your teacher will probably be prepared to negotiate a new deadline. Avoid having to do the whole lot the night before – it's unlikely to be very good.

If disaster strikes, however, and you do find yourself in a crisis, do *something* – anything is better than nothing. Remember that it's easier to get from 0-20 per cent than it is from 60-80 per cent. You could find out if there is any possibility of extending the deadlines. But don't get into this situation too often. You don't want to get a reputation for never handing work in on time. Plan ahead and discipline yourself for coursework. The thing about assessment systems which involve coursework is that they can be much harder than those which don't. Be prepared for this. Unlike exams, you really can't leave it all to the last minute. Organization is the most important thing to remember when it comes to doing coursework. Apart from the unpleasantness of having teachers pursuing you round college for your essay, you won't be able to get all your work done in time if you put it off too much, and then you will fail your exam. Try to complete assignments as they come up. Then with any luck they won't hurt so much. It's rather like tidying your bedroom – if you pick up your clothes as you take them off, you don't have to wade through them by the weekend.

Make the most of your opportunities

Can you decide how many pieces of work you do? If you have to submit a certain number of assignments, that's final – there is nothing you can do about it. But if your course is more flexible, think carefully about what you set yourself. Could you get a better grade by attempting more, or will you just produce poorer work? Ask your teacher's advice. Don't underestimate yourself, but go for quality rather than quantity if you feel you can't produce both.

Can you choose the work you do? If you can choose from a choice of projects, or even make up your own, think carefully about your strengths and weaknesses. Choose things you enjoy doing or are interested in if possible – you may have to spend some time doing them. Some projects may be more difficult than others; on the other hand, if you have a go at a harder question, you may be judged more generously than if you had stuck to one that you knew you could do. Ask your teacher's advice. He or she will have a good knowledge of your abilities and be able to look at them more objectively than you can.

If you have a choice over what you do, talk your decision over with your teacher. Be prepared to negotiate about what you should be doing. If you have very strong feelings about the way you want to do something, make them clear, but be prepared to give a bit if your teacher doesn't think it's a good idea. After all, he or she wants you to do as well as possible.

Can you discuss a project with your teacher while you are doing it? Or are you allowed to discuss it once it is finished? If you can hand in a revised version, make the most of your opportunity to do so. Think about what your teacher has said, then try and put it into practice. Are you happy with the structure of your work? Are there more examples or facts you could include? Do you need to check your spelling and grammar? Have you learnt anything by discussing the assignment in class or with friends, that you could now put in?

GCSE teachers are not allowed to make actual corrections, but they are allowed to give you a general guideline as to the sorts of thing you might be able to improve. So, for instance, your teacher won't say to you, 'You have misspelt this or that word', but may well suggest that you check your spelling in general. That's a pretty good hint that something is wrong! Discuss the structure of your essay with your teacher – does he or she feel it could be better organized? Listen to your teachers – they will be able to give you valuable advice on your work. And do ask for help if you are at all unsure about what you have to do or how you can improve an assignment.

Once you have finished and handed in an assignment, however, don't waste time worrying about mistakes you remember too late. Just remember not to make them again. It's natural for you to see the mistakes and not the good parts, but this is not what an examiner is trained to do.

Teacher problems

Do you feel that your teacher dislikes you and marks your work down unfairly? Remember that this is very unlikely to happen in an assessment – the teacher will want his or her class to get the best marks possible. The assessment reflects on him or her as well as on you! But if you really feel strongly about it, it might be possible to discuss the problem with a more sympathetic teacher.

Vary your coursework

Make sure that you don't give in five identical types of assignment to be assessed. The examiners will be unable to see the other things you are good at. Your teacher should make sure that you try your hand at different things.

Make sure your coursework is well presented

If your work is neat, easy to read and well structured, you are bound to get better marks. Check it through before you give it in, especially for faults in grammar and spelling, and anything that isn't clear.

Here are some different sorts of coursework assignment that you might be expected to complete, and some hints on how best to go about them.

A descriptive report

Most courses will call for some descriptive writing. For instance, in an English language exam you might be asked to write a magazine article on the work of the NSPCC. First you need to get hold of the necessary information – you may be given this, or part of the assignment may be to find it in a library, or by writing to the relevant organization.

Now you have your facts, you need to present all the information so it is clear. Do your sentences lead on from each other logically? Have you included all the relevant information, and does each of your paragraphs deal with a separate theme? Every paragraph should always have one controlling idea. Imagine that you are reading the report – does it tell you everything you would need to know? Does it make sense? Get a friend to read it if you are not sure. Remember you are meant to be describing the situation, not arguing about it. Keep your opinions well out of this sort of piece – there should be plenty of room for them in other areas of writing. And don't just tell the story – keep your information organized in other ways. Pick out key features of the way an organization works, for instance. Use examples and case situations, and don't be afraid to make them up if necessary!

You need to get your tone of voice right – a report of this kind should sound fairly formal. So don't write it in the sort of words you would use to your friends. On the other hand, don't use jargon that will confuse people. Your teacher ought to be able to show you examples of well-written reports that will guide you. If you are working from sources, you should be reproducing the information in different words. Balance your own personal voice with a reasoned tone.

A discussion piece

This might be an essay on the rights and wrongs of abortion. This is probably the most difficult sort of question you will have to do, as your reasoning has to be very organized: make sure that you spend plenty of time on it. You will be using much the same technique as for essay questions, but as you have more time, your argument obviously needs to be fuller, with more examples.

You will need to present both sides of the argument, but your personal response should also come out strongly. So you could structure your general argument as follows:

Some people think that . . .
But I feel that . . .

Use relevant examples, statistics and figures. You should have considered both sides of the argument. Try listening to someone who you know will disagree with you, or read an article by a writer who is opposed to the subject. Look for good examples you could use in newspapers, or in documentary programmes. Part of your homework may be to find out some of the information – ask your teacher where to look, and try magazines, books and special organizations involved with the subject.

You might be asked to do this assignment in the form of a debate – to make a speech for both sides. Make sure your ideas link logically together: read it out to someone if you aren't sure and see that your work makes sense. Using a tape-recorder is also helpful. (Even if this isn't the way that you will finally have to present your work, it is often good practice.)

Alternatively, you might be asked to write a series of letters to magazines, pretending these are from people who would have different opinions on the subject in question. For example, on the abortion question suggested, you might write one letter as from a priest, and one as from a mother with a handicapped child – persons who would have very different thoughts on the subject.

Creative writing
Most of us at some stage have to write a personal or imaginative creative piece, for example, a memory or a reflection, or perhaps a short story. The title might be something like: 'My earliest memory', or 'Describe five different rooms so as to show their inhabitants' characters', or 'A walk in the woods'. It's easier to write well if your imagination is immediately fired by the title. But if it isn't, try thinking carefully about the subject before you start – can you see a new angle to it? If you still can't think of anything it might be worth having a word with your teacher to see if you can't come up with your own title, or at least negotiate something which appeals to you more.

Try to show a good range of descriptive vocabulary and sentence structures in your writing. You want to avoid starting all your sentences in the same way. Try out new words you have come across in class or in books. Make a list of all the sights and smells and sounds you can think of – these are the things which bring an event to life and make it vivid. Try brainstorming if you are stuck – just write down everything you can think of for a minute – then look through what you have got and decide what would be good to use. Be thoughtful – what would make the piece come alive? If it was an event that actually happened, what was it about it that you really remember? How did you feel? How did the other people concerned feel? Use comparisons – what was it like? But try and avoid using clichés; your teacher will soon point them out if you do.

Always plan before you write. And remember to have a beginning, a middle and an end – structure is very important and it is something that students tend to forget about in creative writing. The beginning is especially vital. It should be memorable and interesting: your aim is to get the reader hooked at the start of the story. Try and keep it simple, you haven't room in the length you are aiming at to introduce too many characters and events. Similarly, don't just concentrate on plot – make sure you have description as well as action. Look at the characters' emotions as well as what they did. Remember that in a creative piece you have to write everything down. Whereas the TV can show you a lot about the characters by expressions on their faces and their surroundings, a written story has to put all these things into words. Write about things you know, you will sound more convincing that way. And you will have the information necessary to go into detail about an experience.

A comprehension question done under controlled circumstances
This is like a mini-exam, and as in exams, the most important thing to remember is not to panic. Read the passage several times, and make notes about it if you like. It might be a poem, or an extract from a play or a novel, or a historical source, or even a diagram – it depends on the subject. Get a good idea of what it is about. Then turn to the questions and read those several times, thinking of how they apply to the text. (If you look at the questions before you have fully read the passage, you are much more likely to panic.)

The questions will start off easier and get harder. The first few will probably ask quite straightforward factual questions. Make sure that you get your information from all of the text, not just from a particular sentence. You may find out more about the question if you read to the end. The next set of questions will probably ask you to think a bit more carefully about the passage – to read between the lines a little. Try to back up your answers with short quotations from the text. The third sort of question will demand a more imaginative sort of response. You might be asked to imagine you were a character in the passage and describe the events from his or her point of view. Think about the character's thoughts and feelings, don't just give a plot summary.

In this sort of timed paper, make sure that you are answering the question. Keep looking at it to make sure that you are! Check any marks indicated in brackets for a guide to what is wanted: if the question carries two marks, for example, you will need to mention two separate things. Don't repeat information from answer to answer, it shouldn't be needed. Remember to write neatly and check everything through for spelling and grammar before you give it in.

Group work discussion

Some courses will assess you on discussion in class. The group might be given a problem to solve through discussion. Remember that this isn't a competition to say the most or the best. You will need to be able to show that you can co-operate and work for the good of the group. Listening is very important. It is your responsibility to include and draw out the quieter people in the group. Learn not to interrupt other people, tempting as it may be! The people who do badly in this sort of exercise are those who don't listen, who come out only with their own ideas, talk nonstop, or behave rudely to other people. If you are asked to be the group chairperson, you will need to be extra considerate and take everyone into account. You might also be asked to have a discussion in pairs – this is usually easier, especially if you are with a friend.

Remember that you may be assessed at any time in class, so be on your guard. Usually, however, the teacher will pick a time when you are doing well. If you never normally do well, you may have to attend a special assessment session, which will probably be more painful. In GCSE it pays to keep up a steady standard in class.

Questions which ask you to use your imagination

Another new sort of question often included on GCSE papers asks you to make an imaginative response to a situation: 'Imagine you are a soldier in the Battle of Bannockburn', 'Imagine you are Lady Macbeth', 'Continue the Third Act'. Don't worry about these, just let your imagination range freely. Ask yourself some questions about the character concerned: Why does he behave in this way? How would you feel in this situation? What should she have done? Often candidates who don't do too well overall score comparatively highly on these questions, so don't panic about them.

11
Orals and Other Special Exams

Special sorts of examination
The sorts of thing you may be asked to do in an exam can vary a lot
and it's as well to be prepared for that. Don't just assume that you
will be presented with the traditional three-hour paper. Find out
exactly what you will be expected to do. This chapter looks at the
special sorts of exam that you are likely to encounter, and the
special approaches and special methods of preparation that are
required to deal with them.

Orals
Many students find oral exams even more nerve-racking than
traditional ones. Remember, though, that they are simply an
alternative – some subjects are impossible to test without them.
There is no need to be twice as apprehensive. There are even
students who do better in orals than in written exams. The interviewer will not be trying to trick you, and he or she knows that you
are nervous and will make allowances. Usually, an interviewer will
not even show approval or disapproval, but will simply pass on to
the next question. Don't worry if there is a tape recorder, it will
only be there to make things fairer, not to record your answer so it
can be scanned for every mistake. Remember that there is no need
to answer every question immediately; take your time and try to
relax. Talk a little before you go in, to warm up and prevent your
throat from drying up completely.

Oral exams in foreign languages
In GCSE exams the examiner will probably just be your teacher, so
there is no need to panic. For other exams you may have an outside
examiner, but this shouldn't be too alarming. You won't be

expected to come up with a perfect accent, and there is usually plenty of opportunity beforehand to prepare the topics which will come up: your hobbies, your family and friends, your school, and so on. Practise answers to questions such as 'Do you have any brothers and sisters?' or 'What do you do in your spare time?' Make sure that you don't come up with one-word answers – try to expand a bit. For instance, if you are asked, 'Is your home near your school?', don't just say, 'No', say 'No, I have to take the bus every morning.' If you don't have the vocabulary to tell the exact truth, you can always be inventive. For instance, if you are a champion mouth organ player, and you can't remember the word when you are asked if you play a musical instrument, say you play the piano. They won't check! You need a good imagination, though – you might be asked more about your piano playing or whatever bogus hobby you have taken up. Avoid using too many untranslatable English words, for example names of places or famous personalities or friends or TV programmes – this won't show that you know the language.

For more advanced orals, there is usually a list of topics to prepare, so you can learn all the necessary vocabulary for, say, discussing the unemployment problem in Northern Ireland. Think of questions that might be asked and practise answering them. Try to read widely: remember that an interviewer can ask further questions, unlike an exam paper! Have sessions chatting in the relevant language with friends, and try talking about the issues that will come up.

Oral exams in your own language
These will probably be assessed by your own teacher if you are taking GCSE, which is reassuring. But if it is an external examiner, don't panic. He or she will be judging you in much the same way as your teacher would. You can be assessed on a wide range of activities. These might include the following:

Giving a talk
You might have to choose the subject, talk for a short time about it and then answer questions, to be asked by both the teacher and the other students. Remember to choose a subject that you know something about or feel strongly on, otherwise you won't sound very convincing. Make sure you know what you are going to say

and that your ideas follow logically in sequence, but don't just read out a prepared text – if you do, your talk will sound flat, boring and unspontaneous. Vary your tone of voice, so it doesn't all come out the same, and speak slowly and clearly. Try to include some small jokes – not too riotous – to keep your listeners' attention. Visual aids and posters help with this too. Practise your talk on your friends. Can they hear you clearly? Are you keeping their attention?

When it comes to the questions at the end of your talk, give *detailed* answers to questions. The assessor will want to see that you can talk spontaneously as well as give a prepared speech. If you don't know the answer to a factual question, admit it, but try to mention a place or a book where the answer could be looked up instead.

Reading a passage aloud
If you are given a passage to read, you will probably have a short time to look at it beforehand. Use this time constructively. Think about what the words mean and about the whole character of the piece. Is it humorous or serious, straight or sarcastic? Reflect this in the tone of your voice as you read. Read slowly and clearly and vary your tone. Check you know how to pronounce all the difficult words – if you are given something to prepare well in advance you could practise on someone. Do use movement if it feels natural to you. Just be yourself.

Making a video
This is a good group exercise. Make sure that everyone in the group gets a fair chance to be involved in everything – being the director, acting, producing, stage managing and so on. Your teacher will probably see that you swap round regularly. Be careful about your presentation.

Role-playing
This is where you have to imagine that you are a character in a certain situation, suggested to you by your teacher. Some courses will assess you on your ability to do this. The classic example is to pretend to be taking a pair of faulty shoes back to the shop where they were bought. But at any rate you will probably have to imagine that you are in some sort of conflict situation. You might be trying

to get your neighbour to turn down his loud music late at night, for example, or persuading your parents to let you go camping. The marks here will be for portraying character convincingly, for thinking yourself into other people's situations. Take them seriously! It's all too easy to slip out of character, or to start playing for laughs if all your friends are there. That won't get you any marks. If two of you are involved, don't hog all the conversation. And don't get stuck in Punch and Judy situations when you are playing a conflict: 'Oh yes you did', 'Oh no I didn't'. Try to get the conversation a bit further by mentioning other issues.

Debates

Discuss your debating subject with as many people as possible beforehand to get ideas, and to be warned what sort of line your opponent might take. In the real thing, remember which side of the argument you are on! If you are really stuck, there are books available on debating which may give you some ideas. Try your local library. One example is *Pros and Cons: A Debater's Handbook* by Michael D. Jacobson (Routledge Publishers) which includes entries on advertising, animal rights, capital punishment, the Channel Tunnel, and other likely subjects.

24 hour papers – or more

These are exam papers you do at home, in a set period of time, with your books around you. Such papers may often have a word limit. Make sure that you don't exceed it, and on no account quote excessively from other books, or just paraphrase them for pages and pages. The examiner wants to see what ideas *you* come up with. Try not to work all night – you will get tired and your ideas will wilt. Talk to other people about the questions if you feel it will help you to sort out your ideas, but you should probably avoid the company of people taking the same exam, as they will probably get you into a panic with how much they seem to know. Don't try to read books from scratch, there really isn't time. Use old notes and essays if you need to come up with more material.

Aural exams

Make sure you know the difference between aurals and orals – the first is to do with the ears and the second with the mouth! The two areas you are most likely to have aural exams in are modern languages and music. Again, the thing to do is to listen to practice tapes so that you won't be thrown. Make sure that you listen to a variety of situations.

In language comprehension exams, don't just listen to your teacher, who may not be a native of the country in question, and who may speak slowly for your benefit. Try instead to listen to recordings of native speakers, or TV films or the radio of the country if you can get it in England. Make a trip to the country if at all possible, and listen to as many different people speaking as you can. Try to listen to conversations and passages of about the right length. Remember that the recording may be more colloquial and idiomatic than your textbook. Try to get the general sense first, then you will find that the details slot themselves into place.

For music, practise answering questions about tunes and rhythms played on a variety of instruments – your teacher may play them all on the piano, but the examination tape probably won't. Have a go at writing down from passages from records played at home. In the exam, don't be put off if the rhythm for you to write down is played on jungle drums with a human bone – it is the same rhythm that you would hear on the piano!

Open book exams

These are exams which allow you to bring in your own books or notes, or which provide blank copies of the texts you will need. Be careful not to be overconfident in this sort of exam. You need more preparation, not less. You will have to be able to find your way with great speed through whatever material you are allowed, and that means knowing it very well. If you are given a different edition from the one you normally use, make sure you are familiar with it. Know your way around your notes – make sure that they are well organized, with clear headings. Anything you already know will save you time, so the more preparation you can do the better. It is often wise to treat these exams as if they were ordinary ones, then you can use the open book facility as an extra advantage, rather than it becoming a disadvantage because it slows you down. One big advantage of open book exams, however, is that you can concentrate on learning the main points. As long as you know precisely where specific formulae, quotations, or examples are to be found, you needn't waste your valuable time learning their exact form.

Science practicals

Remember that your practical will probably be asking you to analyse your result as well as simply perform the experiment. Record everything neatly, and notice where the emphasis is put on the question. Pace yourself well – it's all too easy to run out of time. For identification exams, look at as many specimens as possible beforehand so that you know what they might come up with – you need to be familiar with the range of possibilities. Get your teachers or other students to set up practice tests for you. If you have to use a microscope, make sure that your eyesight is all right and if you wear glasses that they are clean and right for you. If the microscope is out of focus, ask the invigilator or supervisor to reset it – don't fiddle with it yourself. You need to be particularly organized in preparing for these exams as you need to work in a special place. Make sure that you can get to the lab sufficiently to revise; the night before won't do, as it will probably be shut, or at the least overcrowded with last minute revisers.

Art exams

Art exams will be looking for originality of composition as much as brilliance of execution. What you decide to draw and how to arrange it is as important as how you draw it. Try to think of a new angle on the subject – be imaginative and experiment in your preliminary sketches with as many ways of doing the painting as possible. You may well have to give in these sketches as part of your exam. If you do, make sure that they are well presented.

The most frustrating thing about art exams is the time limit, and it is this which is the stumbling block for many students. Make sure that you can finish in the time. The best way to do this is to prepare as much as you possibly can before. Try out what you decide to do beforehand so that you don't run into unforeseen problems in the actual exam. It's very hard to change your mind halfway through, and you probably won't finish if you do.

Cookery exams

First, and this is most important, devote ten minutes or so to working out a good time plan. Its no use realising half an hour before the exam ends that you've still got to make a dish which takes over an hour to cook. If you are doing the sort of cookery exam where you know in advance what you are going to cook, then learn the recipes off by heart. This way you will save time by not having to refer continually to a cookery book.

Get all your equipment set out before the exam starts, and always use the right tool for the right job. Feeling that you can save time by making one kind of knife, for example, do two different jobs can lead to mistakes and get you into a panic. Plan right at the beginning which serving dishes you are going to use, and clear up and wash up as you go along. This not only gives you more space to work in, but makes you look and feel more efficient.

Keep an eye on the clock, especially towards the end of the exam. Tell yourself that it is going to finish twenty minutes before it really does, and then you won't find yourself trying to do an impossible amount of things in the last five minutes. Time always goes very quickly at the end of a cookery exam.

Finally, don't forget to keep tasting as you go along.

12

Health and Strength

Exams are physically and mentally exhausting. So it makes sense to take care of yourself beforehand. You won't do your best if you allow yourself to get overanxious and run down. Bear the following points in mind throughout your revision campaign.

Morale

Morale – in the sense of 'I believe I am going to do well' – is half the battle and the whole of what this chapter is about. So believe it, really believe it! The simple techniques of assertion, regularly repeated – 'All is well. All is going well. All is going to go well' – should not be sneered at. They are powerful magic.

Keep cheerful! If you find it difficult to be cheerful, pretend to be cheerful, and behave as though you *were* cheerful. Sing, dance, laugh, consult your favourite joke book: and the spirit will follow the flag.

Food

Take breaks from your work to have proper meals – exam candidates, like armies, march on their stomachs. If you stop eating properly you will feel tired much more quickly and lower your resistance to all kinds of infection, and this is the worst possible time for you to be ill.

Don't start a diet just before the exams – it will take your mind off your work. Instead, you should try to eat a balanced diet with plenty of fresh fruit and green vegetables, white meat and fish, potatoes, rice, pasta, beans, and so on. Healthy food can be psychologically helpful too – you can feel that you are feeding yourself up for the great endeavour. Multivitamin tablets and those fizzy vitamin C tablets are useful for this too. Don't change your eating habits drastically before exams as you want to avoid any risk of medical problems.

If you are foraging for yourself, it may be tempting to live on quick snacks from takeaways to save time, but try to avoid too much junk food over long periods. Go for the healthier options instead – filled baked potatoes, for instance, or the quick meals and ready-prepared salads that most supermarkets stock nowadays. Or find a cheap restaurant. On the other hand, if you are planning a head-down two-week marathon revision campaign, junk food may be just what you need and it won't harm you for a short period of time.

Drink
Alcohol in small amounts can be very relaxing at the end of a revision session, and the treat of going out to the pub for last orders can compensate for a long evening in. In larger amounts, however, it can give you terrible hangovers which prevent you from working efficiently and rot your body in the long term. Know your limits! And beware of using drink to blot out your exam worries – they will still be there in the morning, and a hangover will make them seem worse than ever. Don't drink at all the night before the actual exam, it's not worth the risk. Save it for when they're all over.

Smoking
If you smoke, this probably isn't the time for you to give it up. You will be more tense and irritable than usual anyway, and withdrawal symptoms will play havoc with your concentration. But make sure you can go for three hours or however long is necessary without having to have a cigarette to calm yourself down. You don't want to waste valuable exam time smoking in the lavatory.

Coffee and other drugs
Most students find that they are pretty dependent on coffee when it comes to revising for exams. It's not only the caffeine that keeps you going, it's that wonderful break while you boil the kettle and wash up a mug. You can drink a fair amount of coffee a day without any serious ill effects, but watch out if you start to feel too jittery and hyperactive, because this won't help you concentrate. It also messes up your sleep patterns. Try changing to decaffeinated coffee and see if it helps.

Beware of stronger drugs during exam periods. Some students swear by concentrated caffeine tablets, but they shouldn't be necessary. If you haven't mastered the exam subject by now, you won't do it by staying up all night for weeks at a time. You really need to be at your best physically. Speed and amphetamines do nothing for your exam technique: although they may convince *you* you are doing wonderfully at the time, the actual results are rather different. Don't take any but prescribed medicines, and remember that tranquillizers can produce highly undesirable side effects in some people including a tendency to sluggish thinking – the last thing you want at this time.

Exercise
There is no need to run half a marathon daily, but do try to take some exercise. A sport you enjoy, or a dance class, jogging or even a short walk in the park can take your mind off your worries amazingly well. Physical activity, particularly in the open air, is a great stress-beater, especially when you have been cooped up over your desk for too long. Even a stretch between revision sessions can help.

Going out
You will need to go out and enjoy yourself sometimes, or you will go mad instead! Nobody can work all the time. In fact, if you don't take any breaks, your work will suffer. But try to ration yourself, and use a night out as a reward for a revision session achieved. That way you will enjoy yourself more anyway.

Sleep
Many students do experience problems with sleep during exam periods – it's nothing unusual. Try having a hot milky drink before you go to bed, and give yourself some time to unwind after a work session – read a magazine or watch TV. Avoid drinking coffee in the evening if you find you can't sleep. A hot bath is soporific too, and diverts the blood from the brain to the skin.

If you are still having problems, you might want to try other remedies, such as homoeopathic or stronger drugs, but do consult your doctor beforehand, and make sure he or she knows you are taking exams. You don't want to take anything that will make you feel drugged or sleepy during the daytime. Above all, try not to worry too much about not sleeping – there is nothing more likely to prevent you from dropping off. The human body can do amazingly well on astonishingly little amounts of sleep, so as long as you are not suffering from insomnia for too long, you should be all right. But do see a doctor if you are worried.

Relaxation
Make sure that you have frequent breaks from your revision. How you relax, and how well you relax, will depend considerably upon how well you know yourself. It might be worthwhile to make a list of brief 'interlude' activities that you know from experience to be helpful: meditation, deep breathing, yoga or some specific exercise, the reading or recitation of a particular text or quotation, playing a musical instrument, painting or sketching, taking a stroll in the fresh air, looking at some particular view or picture, listening to the news, a favourite piece of music or radio programme, reading a magazine . . . Variety is part of the solution. What is important is that what you choose should work for you without being too time consuming.

You may find special relaxation techniques useful: try some of the relaxation tapes that are available now, or try the following exercise:

Find yourself a space well away from your revision place. Lie down on the floor and distance yourself mentally from your work. Now, starting from your feet, consciously tense and relax each part of your body, your toes, your whole foot, your shins, your thighs . . . until you reach your head. Then tense and relax your whole body. You should be so limp that your arm can be picked up and let fall to the floor with no resistance: try this with a friend.

Tension
Taking exams makes people whingeing, bad-tempered and self-obsessed. Make sure that your family and friends know why you are being so horrible, so that they can sympathize and be nice to you. Be nice to them afterwards.

Extreme stress
If you find that you are getting unreasonably depressed and anxious, consult your teacher, or if necessary your doctor, *now*. Some people do find that they have extreme reactions to exams –

it's nothing to be ashamed of. And the sooner you get help, the sooner you will be able to sort out your problems. Remember that exam stress is a temporary state – you will soon be yourself again.

Illness

If you are ill during your revision period, take care of yourself. Stop working, see a doctor and go to bed until you feel better. You won't do any useful work if you are ill, and it will take you longer to recover if you keep pushing yourself. If you are ill for a long time, consult your teacher about what to do. You may want to put off the exam, or it may be necessary to write to the exam board and explain the circumstances.

See your doctor before the exam about any problems you think you will have, such as hayfever, colds or period pains. You should be able to get drugs to prevent or alleviate these during the exam. If you *are* ill during the actual exam, it is probably as well to keep going if at all possible – you may do better than you think. Write to the exam board immediately afterwards to tell them that you were ill in the exam.

Conclusion

It may have occurred to you that this book is really just a list of questions to ask yourself. Exams are about asking yourself questions, and then coming up with the right answers. Don't wait for the examiner to ask you the questions – ask the questions yourself first.

Taking an exam asks you to sum up a situation and then to produce what is most appropriate for it, to the best of your abilities. You don't have to do your best work ever, in fact, it's most unlikely that in three hours under exam conditions you will even come up to your normal standard. Adrenalin can do a lot for you, letting you think far harder than you would normally be able to, but the fact remains that exam answers are always scrappier than those produced as coursework.

This doesn't matter. Examiners are trained to take exam pressures into account. They know nobody can produce a beautifully polished piece of work in forty minutes. Instead they look for a good grasp of facts and an intelligent approach to the question. Your examiner will mark your paper quickly – examiners are busy people and they don't waste time looking for the faults. Don't brood over finished exam paper. You will never see that embarrassingly bad essay again.

Once you have finished your exams, try as hard as you can to put them out of your mind. Don't indulge in those agonizing post-mortems with other students, when you realize that you forgot to turn over the paper and didn't attempt half the questions. Don't compare answers and find that while your answer to Number 7 was '400xy/17', every else seems to have come up with '2'.

When the results come out, you may well be surprised at how well you have done, all things considered. If you aren't, don't despair. If an exam result is very important to you, you can usually take it again. And believe it or not, what you learn about handling and recalling information by taking exams will be as useful to you as any number of good results.

Let's admit it, exams can be something of a lucky draw. Every time the results come out, there will be people who have done surprisingly well or surprisingly badly. But the more sensible preparation you are able to do, the more likely you are to be in there when they are handing out the goodies, rather than scrabbling about at the bottom of the dusty bin. Best of luck! Now get back to your revision and stop putting things off.

Appendix I

List of Examination Boards

East Anglian Examinations Board,
The Lindens,
Lexden Road,
Colchester CO3 3RL
(Tel: 0206 549595)

London Regional Examining Board,
Lyon House,
104 Wandsworth High Street,
London SW18 4LF
(Tel: 01 870 2144)

University of London School Examinations Board,
Stewart House,
32 Russell Square,
London WC1B 5DP
(Tel: 01 636 8000)

East Midland Regional Examinations Board,
Robins Wood House,
Robins Wood Road,
Aspley,
Nottingham
NG8 3NR
(Tel: 0602 296021)

Oxford and Cambridge Schools Examinations Board,
10 Trumpington Street,
Cambridge CB2 1QB
(Tel: 0223 64326)

Oxford and Cambridge Schools Examinations Board,
Elsfield Way,
Oxford OX2 8EP
(Tel: 0865 54421)

Southern Universities Joint Board,
Cotham Road,
Cotham,
Bristol BS6 6DD
(Tel: 0272 736042)

The West Midlands Examinations Board,
Norfolk House,
Smallbrook Queensway,
Birmingham B5 4NJ
(Tel: 021 631 2151)

University of Cambridge Local Examinations Syndicate,
Syndicate Buildings,
1 Hills Road,
Cambridge CB1 2EU
(Tel: 0223 61111)

Associated Lancashire Schools Examining Board,
12 Harter Street,
Manchester M1 6HL
(Tel: 061 228 0084)

Joint Matriculation Board,
Manchester M15 6EU
(Tel: 061 273 2565)

Northern Regional Examinations Board
Wheatfield Road
Westerhope
Newcastle upon Tyne NE5 5JZ
(Tel: 091 286 2711)

North West Regional Examinations Board,
Orbit House,
Albert Street,
Eccles,
Manchester M30 0WL
(Tel: 061 788 9521)

Yorkshire and Humberside Regional Examinations Board,
31-33 Springfield Avenue,
Harrogate,
North Yorkshire,
HG1 2HW
(Tel: 0423 566991)

Yorkshire and Humberside Regional Examinations Board,
Scarsdale House,
136 Derbyshire Lane,
Sheffield S8 8SE
(Tel: 0742 557436)

Northern Ireland Schools Examinations Council,
Beechill House,
42 Beechill Road,
Belfast BT8 4RS
(Tel: 0232 704666)

Associated Examining Board,
Stag Hill House,
Guildford,
Surrey GU2 5XJ
(Tel: 0483 506506)

South East Regional Examinations Board,
2-10 Mount Ephraim Road,
Tunbridge Wells,
Kent TN1 1EU
(Tel: 0892 35311/2/3/4)

Southern Regional Examination Board,
Avondale House,
33 Carlton Crescent,
Southampton SO9 4YL
(Tel: 0703 32312)

The South Western Examinations Board,
23-29 Marsh Street,
Bristol BS1 4BP
(Tel: 0272 273434)

University of Oxford Delegacy of Local Examinations,
Ewert Place,
Banbury Road,
Summertown,
Oxford OX2 7BZ
(Tel: 0865 54291)

Welsh Joint Education Committee,
245 Western Avenue,
Cardiff CF5 2YX
(Tel: 0222 561231)

Appendix II

Useful Addresses

Advisory Centre for Education (ACE)
18 Victoria Park Square
London E2 9BP
(Tel: 01 980 4596)

Business and Technician Education Council (BTEC)
Central House
Upper Woburn Place
London WC1H 0HH
(Tel: 01 388 3288)

Career Analysts
Career House
90 Gloucester Place
London W1H 4BH
(Tel: 01 935 5452)

Career and Educational Counselling
Tavistock Centre
120 Belsize Lane
London NW3 5BA
(Tel: 01 794 1309)

Careers Research and Advisory Centre (CRAC)
Bateman Street
Cambridge CB2 1LZ
(Tel: 0223 460277)

City and Guilds of London Institute
76 Portland Place
London W1N 4AA
(Tel: 01 580 3050)

Department of Education and Science
Elizabeth House
York Road
London SE1 7PH
(Tel: 01 934 9000)

Further Education Information Services (FEIS)
Room 531
Elizabeth House
York Road
London SE1 7PH
(Tel: 01 934 9000)

National Institute of Adult Continuing Education (NIAE)
(England and Wales)
196 De Montford Street
Leicester LE1 7GE
(Tel: 0533 551451)

National Union of Students
461 Holloway Road
London N7 6LJ
(Tel: 01 272 8900)

The Open University
Walton Hall
Milton Keynes MK7 6AA
(Tel: 0908 274066)

Polytechnics Central Admission System (PCAS)
P.O. Box 67
Cheltenham
Glos. GL50 3AP
(Tel: 0242 526225)

Royal Society of Arts Examination Board
8 John Adam Street
London WC2 6EZ
(Tel: 01 930 5115)

Scottish Institute of Adult and Continuing Education (SIACE)
30 Rutland Square
Edinburgh EH1 2BW
(Tel: 031 229 0331)

Universities Central Council on Admissions (UCCA)
P.O. Box 28
Cheltenham
Glos. GL50 1HY
(Tel: 0242 222444)

University of Buckingham
Buckingham
MK18 1EG
(Tel: 0280 914080)
(The University of Buckingham is independent of state finance and processes its own admissions.)

Workers' Educational Association (WEA)
9 Upper Berkeley Street
London W1H 9BY
(Tel: 01 402 5608)